WITHDRAWN

MARIAN UNIVERSITY LIBRARY
INDIANAPOLIS, IN

Page 1. A stained-glass window in the choir loft of The National Shrine of the Immaculate Conception features the shield of the Archdiocese of Boston. The Shrine is the largest Catholic church in the Western Hemisphere and the world's eighth largest.

Pages 2-3. The Shrine's gleaming Byzantine-style dome, bearing symbols of Mary, overlooks several University buildings. From left: Caldwell Hall, home of the School of Religious Studies; Hannan Hall, home to the physics department and Vitreous State Laboratory; and McMahon Hall, which houses the schools of Philosophy and Arts and Sciences.

Pages 4-5. The University in 1928 purchased these volumes belonging to the Albani family of Urbino, of which Pope Clement XI was a member. The books are among 10,000 volumes in the Clementine Library, a collection of rare 15th- to 18th-century books housed in the John K. Mullen of Denver Memorial Library.

Pages 6-7. Celebrating commencement are students, members of the faculty, families and friends of the Columbus School of Law. Established in 1898, the school offers day and evening divisions to a highly select student body.

Below. Architectural detail of the facade of McMahon Hall, which opened in 1895.

Acknowledgments

A conversation at lunch with Father William J. Byron, S.J., and Vincent Walter, secretary of the University, in 1986 became the cornerstone upon which this book was built. To them both and to Anne Smith, I am indebted for the freedom and encouragement that permitted this personal interpretation of our University. Anne Smith and her Public Affairs staff, including Maureen Stotland and John Rich, labored hard to research and write most of the captions that accompany photographs. Saro Dedeyan set up many appointments for me and never hesitated to lend a hand with my equipment.

My tireless photographic assistants were John Wiltse, Jennifer Wondries, Donnie Norwood, Rimas Simonaitis, and CUA's former Public Affairs photographer, Nick Crettier. My children Marc, Anne, Sophia and Paul filled in when all else failed.

Jack Beveridge's unique talent for design has brilliantly placed the photographs and type. Charles O. Hyman generously contributed his time and extraordinary vision to correct the color separations that translated my photographs to ink on paper.

To all the professors who willingly cooperated with me, no matter what disruptive influence my lights and presence created in their classrooms—my sincere thanks. I am especially grateful to those students who, often unwittingly, became the focus of my camera and thereby helped to make this book a true mirror of the University.

Bill Graham and his Department of Drama provided the subject matter that has exhilarated me since my student days, when the legendary Father Gilbert V. Hartke welcomed me and my camera into the magical world of the theater, and I discovered the excitement of photographing actors and actresses on stage. Robert Ricks and his orchestra of student musicians were wonderful to listen to and inspired me to try to match my art with theirs. To the athletics department and all the coaches and athletes, you'll always be winners in my book.

Finally to the co-author in all my efforts, my wife Suzy, who organized and cataloged the thousands of slides I produced and read through my drafts for the introduction with gentle severity—my loving thanks.

Fred J. Maroon

Century Ended, Century Begun:
The Catholic University of America
Fred J. Maroon
Photography and Introduction by Fred J. Maroon
Foreword by William J. Byron, S.J.

Designed by Jack Beveridge
Edited by Anne B. Smith

Copyright © 1990 by The Catholic University of America Press. Photographs and introductions Copyright © 1990 by Fred J. Maroon. All rights reserved. This book, or any portion thereof, may not be reproduced in any form without permission of the publisher, The Catholic University of America Press. Photographs and introduction may not be reproduced in any form without permission of Fred J. Maroon.

Published by The Catholic University of America Press.
The Catholic University of America, Washington, D.C. 20064.
Printed in the United States by Hoechstetter. First edition.

Library of Congress Cataloging-in-Publication Data
Maroon, Fred J.
  Century ended, century begun: The Catholic University of America/ Fred J. Maroon; photography and introduction by Fred J. Maroon; foreword by William J. Byron, S.J.
    p. cm.
  ISBN 0-8132-0735-5.
    1. Catholic University of America–Pictorial works.
    2. Catholic University of America–Anniversaries, etc. I. Title.
LD843.M37 1990
378.753–dc20   90-36773
                    CIP

THE CATHOLIC UNIVERSITY OF AMERICA PRESS

Century Ended, Century Begun

The Catholic University of America

Fred J. Maroon

Photography and Introduction by Fred J. Maroon

Foreword by William J. Byron, S.J.

Introduction

by Fred J. Maroon

Although the distance from The Catholic University of America to my home in Georgetown is short enough, for me the two are almost a lifetime apart. When in 1986 CUA President William J. Byron, S.J., invited me for a "free lunch," he broached the subject of CUA's upcoming centennial and suggested it would be nice to have a photographic book commemorating this event. Soon after, I was back on the campus that had been my home for four years, 40 years earlier. It was a strange homecoming. There were a number of new buildings, but many old ones remained unchanged. In some corners of the campus it was as though time had stood still. Of course, the University I had known was not just buildings and real estate. It was teachers and classmates. It was my life there as a student.

New Brunswick, N.J., where I was born, was a city of considerable ethnic and religious diversity, but its Catholic community was able to support several elementary and secondary schools. Sacred Heart Grammar School and St. Peter's High School instilled values in me that I assumed were universal: respect for God, home, teachers, community and country. With World War II on and my country at war, graduation from high school could not come soon enough for me. I had been sworn into the Navy a few weeks earlier, and I left for boot camp the day after graduation. At what I now realize was a very tender and innocent age, I was forced to face not only my own possible mortality and the actual loss of a number of my closest friends, but also assaults on the Catholic values and beliefs I had been taught in a relatively sheltered, small-town childhood. Most of my shipmates had not met a Catholic before, and I was constantly being called upon to justify my religion and how my God could allow the things happening in the world at that time. Fortunately, my parents and the Sisters of Charity had done their job well. I had a strong enough arsenal to combat my shipmates' challenges, but the experience left me wanting more substantial answers to questions of my own. At war's end, these were some of the thoughts that accompanied me to CUA, where I pursued an architecture degree.

In September of 1946 universities across the country welcomed the largest freshman class in American history. The class consisted largely of war veterans—mature, worldly, and sometimes scarred. Eager to make up for what we perceived to be lost time and childhoods in the Depression, we were determined to prepare ourselves for careers that would give us better lives than those of our parents. CUA was ready for us, but with its own agenda. It asked us to think about God, the history of man, eternal values and our reasons for being. The University taught us that making a living is not as important as loving what we do and doing it to the best of our abilities. The University introduced us to the great minds and thoughts of the past through the men and women who were our professors. Though I bade them farewell at graduation, they and the values they instilled in me have remained my traveling companions.

Upon returning to the campus in 1986, I found myself surrounded by ghosts and memories. Gone was the Dugout, where just the right number of hours were spent discussing God, truth, beauty, and the girls of Trinity; those who made the Dugout a home earned the undesirable label of "lounge lizards." Graduate Hall, where the Dugout was located, has been extensively enlarged and is known as University Center. A new cafeteria has replaced the old dining room. The only thing that remains unchanged are the jokes about the quality and quantity of the food, or lack thereof. Gone also is the temporary building that housed the architecture department, where we would "charrette"—work 24 hours a day for three days in a row before a design deadline. Charrette time was punctuated only by midnight hikes to the Hot Shoppe on Rhode Island Avenue for coffee, eggs and waffles. The "Old Gym" has been transformed into a state-of-the-art Center for Architectural Studies and named for one of my classmates, Ed Crough. The art department has not changed a bit. It is exactly as it was in 1950. The smell of paint needs only my painting instructor Andrea de Zerega's colorful accent proclaiming: "To paint is the most wonderful thing in the world. Not to paint is one of the worst."

Gibbons Hall was where I lived, and it is still one of the most elegant buildings on campus. For us undergraduates the hall's tower on the Michigan Avenue side was a great platform from which to shout at Trinity girls, in between the roar of the passing trolley cars. The campus side was used mainly for launching missiles and water balloons on unsuspecting victims below. The Tower was also the place from which mascots were

Students from the class of 1950 gather beneath the entrance arch of one place that symbolizes the University—McMahon Hall. From the 1950 *Cardinal*.

hung. One was "Homer," a dummy much loved by Gibbonites. His theft in 1947 by Mount St. Mary's Mountaineers resulted in the playful redecoration of key elements of the Mount St. Mary's campus by a contingent of artistic CUA students wielding pots of red paint. The Mountaineers, overreacting typically to this harmless little prank, descended on CUA with vengeful outrage. The assault had everything. Mountaineers dressed as priests infiltrated our command posts, hoping to prevent an alarm from being sounded. But before the hostilities were over, 400 students were locked in battle on all sides of Gibbons Hall. The Mountaineers whitewashed our campus before they retreated, but our football heroes whitewashed Mount St. Mary's that weekend, 26-0.

Gibbons had everything I needed. I could get the Lord on my side at Mass in the basement chapel each morning. But if the day still didn't go as well as I had hoped there was in the evening a television waiting in the lounge, and I could rely on Steve Allen, Red Skelton, or Sid Caesar to turn things around for me. My oversized bedroom in the Tower, which I shared with long-suffering Bob Nolte, doubled as the darkroom where I developed and enlarged all the photographs for the *Cardinal* yearbook. It was also a hangout for neighbors Charlie Hummel and Herm Terzino, and whoever wandered in.

Looking back, I realize those bull sessions were as much a part of our education as our academic studies, and the sessions also provided a good balance for a relatively heavy workload. Because of the war, the traditional five-year architecture program had been condensed into four. This left little time for electives, but those on the Dean's List were allowed to take one. My parish priest in New Brunswick exhorted me not to miss what he considered to be one of the best opportunities a student at CUA could have. According to him, my education would be incom-

Left. Tubes and wires surround students who boil and bubble, toil and trouble. From the 1950 *Cardinal*.

Above. A design project for a city library occupies architecture majors Owen Hendon and Harry Dierken, who with Herm Terzino were layout editors for the 1950 *Cardinal*.

plete without Father Charles Hart's course on metaphysics. I signed up eagerly in my junior year, and it immediately became evident that three years of convoy duty in the North Atlantic were insufficient preparation for the kind of metaphysics on Father Hart's mind. He referred to those whose opinions he did not respect as "having their feet firmly planted in the clouds." I empathized with them. But while I may not have gotten as much out of the class as some, it did answer some of those questions I had brought with me as a freshman.

In the spring of my junior year my class elected me editor of the *Cardinal* yearbook. I never dreamed that photography, my hobby since I was 12, and that yearbook would change my life's plans. Our dedicated, hard-working staff produced a yearbook that won the top award in its class at the National Annual Yearbook Competition. As luck would have it, we used the same engraver as *Life* magazine and our yearbook caught the eye of *Life*'s art director. Shortly before my graduation in 1950, he wrote and asked me to call him if I wanted to work for *Life*. Did I ever! Joe Judge, who wrote the text for the 1950 *Cardinal*, and I spent three months in New York City as editorial assistants. As exciting and seductive as that was, I wasn't ready to turn my back on the career for which I had prepared. *Life* magazine assigned me as a stringer for its Paris bureau while I pursued further architecture studies at l'École Superieure des Beaux Arts, and when the year was up, I returned to practice architecture in the States. Before too long, however, the tail was wagging the dog again, and my hobby became my profession—this time for good.

I was fortunate that this was the era of the "big" magazines. My mentors were some of the greatest editors of the day at *Life*, *Look* and *Holiday*. It was also the beginning of the jet age, enabling editors to send photographers to the remote corners of the world. I needed only a week to reach Outer Mongolia; Marco Polo had a much more arduous journey. Often as I traveled the people found me as much an object of curiosity as I found them. I will never forget the small Irish boy, the spokesman for his inquisitive little band of friends, who timidly approached me to ask: "Excuse me, sir, but are you a stranger from a far and distant land?"

Winter noon is a harsh time of day, as one emerges from the Byzantine gloom of the library lobby to the hard, brittle sunlight. From the 1950 *Cardinal*.

I am often asked if my architecture training has influenced my photography, and of course it has. Architecture studies, in addition to providing a professional degree, offered a great liberal arts education. I studied the history of architecture and of the civilizations responsible, and when magazines assigned me to go to Turkey or Egypt or Rome, I took a frame of reference that has stood me in good stead. I had studied light and shadow, perspective, proportion and the relationship of elements. These are also elements of photographic images. Mathematics, philosophy and literature were required courses for me at CUA. When I began to produce photographic essays and books, I found those disciplines provided the fundamentals for the research, evaluation and organization necessary before a single picture could be taken.

Starting a book on any new subject always fills me with foreboding, but coming back to CUA to do a "sequel" of the *Cardinal* proved terrifying. My first visits to campus with my camera in 1986 did more for Kodak than me. This book was clearly going to require more discipline than any of my eight others. For one thing, I had none of the usual professional support I am used to working with, and my equipment now is too heavy and complex for me to use alone. Also, my other professional responsibilities often prevented the kind of continuity and momentum that such projects require. Once, earlier in my career, I had revisited my past. I spent four years doing the book *Keepers of the Sea* on today's Navy. I was 18 again. The smell of the sea, the roll of the ship, and the youthfulness of the officers and enlisted men pushed my clock back 35 years. Except for when I looked in the mirror each morning to shave, nothing had changed.

Only briefly, when I began work on the CUA book, did I feel like an outsider. Soon, visiting Hartke Theatre, attending philosophy classes or architecture critiques, walking from Gibbons to McMahon, or sharing the excitement while photographing a football or basketball game, I was inevitably drawn back into the University's life. Halfway into the book I found myself hearing a cheerful "Hello, Mr. Maroon" almost as often as I had once heard "Hi, Fred" 40 years earlier. While I could never rekindle the fire of youth, I began to feel at home again. It was a home I had missed.

Being in a classroom with my camera is like a flashback to my youth, I found. I loved attending freshman philosophy courses again. It was all I could do to keep from participating. An architecture critique was led by my senior design professor, Joe Miller, who still teaches after 40 years. Seeing the Cardinals beat Georgetown at football (basketball would be too much to ever hope for!) was almost as thrilling as watching the Redskins beat the Broncos in the Superbowl.

At this point in my life it is interesting to reflect that my first and latest books have been on The Catholic University of America. They are different. The first was black and white. This new one is in color. The *Cardinal* had simplicity, strength, and the exuberance of young students. This new book is more sophisticated and complex, reflecting the discernment and experience of an older person. In 1950 I had only two lenses on my 4x5 Speed Graphic. Now I need two strong-backed assistants just to carry the vast array of Leica cameras, lenses and lights needed to capture my expanded visual vocabulary on film. Still, the heart of the photographer has changed little. My personality always sends me in search of beauty, and my education has enabled me to define beauty in its broadest sense. It is my good fortune to be able to record with my camera many of civilization's most noble and positive achievements. I truly believe that CUA is numbered among them, and I hope the content of this book reflects that.

I'm grateful that Father Byron invited me to that "free" lunch in 1986, and I hope he'll ask me again in another 40 years. It remains to be seen how I will interpret CUA then, but I promise it will be with a different camera.

Ramsey W.J. Flynn and George T. Dundon fill orders with pep and sparkle in the Dugout—"the finest, worst and only place we had." From the 1950 *Cardinal*.

Foreword

by William J. Byron, s.j.

Monsignor John Tracy Ellis, whose photograph appears in this collection, is a gentleman and a symbol. He is a scholar, of course—widely acclaimed as dean of American Church historians—but also a symbol of what The Catholic University of America wanted to say about itself in selecting "Lamp of Learning, Light of Faith" for its Centennial theme. Monsignor Ellis embodies both learning and faith in an admirable way.

In speaking of the place that has long been his intellectual home, John Tracy Ellis likes to quote John Lancaster Spalding, who, as bishop of Peoria and the person chiefly responsible for the founding of the University, spoke at the laying of the cornerstone of Caldwell Hall, the first building on campus, on May 24, 1888. Spalding said of the University: "It will teach the best that is known and encourage research, it will be at once a scientific institute, a school of culture and a training ground for the business of life; it will educate the minds that give direction to the age; it will be a nursery of ideas, a center of influence."

This unique institution was chartered by the Vatican in 1887 at the request of the Bishops of the United States. Instruction and research began at CUA in 1889 in service, as the inscription on the outer wall of Caldwell Hall puts it, *Deo et Patria*. The "lamp" has been in place for one full century. Its "light" has served well both Church and state through the discovery and communication of knowledge. Behind the lamp and its light stand countless men and women of faith whose minds have, as Spalding hoped, given "direction to the age."

Great minds embodied in persons not pictured in this book are a precious part of CUA's first century. Notable among them are Quasten in theology, Kuttner in canon law, Herzfeld in physics, and social-justice theorist John A. Ryan. Monsignor, later Bishop, Fulton J. Sheen made his academic home in the University's School of Philosophy, as radio listeners nationwide

Monsignor John Tracy Ellis enjoys reading as much as teaching. Known as dean of American Catholic Church historians, he is a professorial lecturer in Church history. He received a CUA doctoral degree in 1930.

16

Before a performance of the musical *Nicholas Nickleby*, patrons gather on the plaza of Hartke Theatre, named for the Rev. Gilbert V. Hartke, the Dominican priest who founded the Department of Drama.

were reminded when they tuned in to "The Catholic Hour" on Sunday evenings throughout the decade of the 1930s.

Young minds and bodies have, of course, always been a part of CUA; they still enliven it today, as Fred Maroon's remarkable photographs attest. The Department of Drama, founded by Dominican Father Gilbert V. Hartke in 1939, continues to keep his spirit alive in the campus theater that bears his famous name. The name of Architecture alumnus Benjamin T. Rome is on the School of Music because of his great love and generous support for the performance-focused center of music education on campus. Civil Engineering alumnus Edward M. Crough applied both treasure and talent to the transformation of the Brookland Gymnasium into a Center for Architectural Studies that bears his name. Because of Mr. Crough's vision and generosity, Professor Stanley Hallet was able, in 1989, to quip, "Architecture is the new sport in the Old Gym!" Photographic evidence in support of this assertion enhances the book you now hold in your hands.

The Old Gym would simply have been older as CUA marked its 100th birthday had it not been for the generosity of Raymond A. DuFour, an alumnus who mixed varsity athletics with undergraduate studies before taking his law degree here in 1936. The Raymond A. DuFour Athletic Center houses our varsity sports programs, encourages intramural play, and invites aging faculty to the pool and workout rooms to demonstrate the truth of the dictum, *mens sana in corpore sano*.

In an era of small-time enrollments, the mid-1930s, when the entire student body numbered only 1,500, CUA played big-time football. In the 1935 season, under Coach Arthur J. "Dutch" Bergman, the Flying Cardinals were, as veteran journalist Jeremiah O'Leary wrote in a retrospective article in *The Washington Times* on Jan. 5, 1990, "loaded with a collection of local high school stars and nearly a dozen big Lithuanian and Polish boys

17

from the coal-mining districts of Pennsylvania." They defeated the University of Mississippi by a score of 20-19 to win the Orange Bowl championship on Jan. 1, 1936. "It is difficult to overstate the wild excitement aroused in the hearts of all area residents, especially the Catholics and people living in the Brookland section of Northeast in the shadow of the campus," O'Leary recalled. "Three thousand people were waiting at Union Station when the train arrived bearing the victorious Cardinal team."

In 1989, Cardinal football drew smaller crowds as it competed successfully (a season record of 8 and 2) in Division III of National Collegiate Athletic Association play. Running-back Karl Kohl won All-American honors that season; all athletes, men and women, in all sports participated in a diverse program with an emphasis on an appropriate balance between athletics and academics in the life of the student-athlete. Academics, of course, have always held both primacy and pride of place in the life of the University.

Established by the body now known as the National Conference of Catholic Bishops to be a graduate and research center, CUA encompasses an impressive array of schools—Arts and Sciences, Engineering and Architecture, Law, Library and Information Science, Music, Nursing, Philosophy, Religious Studies, Social Service, and University College, which offers degree programs for non-traditional students. Virtually all states and close to 100 foreign countries are represented in the current body of 3,200 undergraduate and 3,800 graduate and professional students.

Library holdings number approximately 1.2 million; they are housed in the John K. Mullen of Denver Memorial Library, built in 1928, and in six other on-campus library settings. The wealth of the collection lies mainly in its holdings in biblical studies, religion, theology, canon law, early Christian and medieval studies, Greek and Latin texts, Semitic languages, and 19th-century Luso-Brazilian culture and history. The 10,000-volume library of Pope Clement XI, regarded by scholars as a window on the Renaissance and its intellectual life, is, as the *Smithsonian* magazine put it, "enshrined" at CUA along with many other rare book treasures.

Fred Maroon's photographs of the buildings and the people, the places and persons that are CUA today, convey an unmistakable note of optimism that accompanies the University into its second century. Although wonders have been worked here over the past 100 years—wonders in the development of human potential, wonders in the discovery of self, of truth, and of God—we acknowledge that our success in meeting our high ideals has been limited. We stand humbly in the face of an uncertain future. Unknown challenges lie ahead, of course; they raise

Fullback Karl Kohl, a finance major from Williamstown, N.J., picks up yardage during a 58-18 rout of Siena College and sets University rushing records.

The "lamp of learning" lights the way to the physics department in Hannan Hall. Dedicated in 1987, the building's name honors Archbishop Philip M. Hannan of New Orleans, alumnus and former CUA board chairman.

questions worth pondering as one savors the pictures presented here, pictures taken over a four-year span as CUA's first century drew to a close and its second century began. What will the next few generations of students study at CUA? More important, what will they learn?

Some will come to prepare themselves to participate in the application of technology to services. Some will want to participate in the development of the new technologies that others will apply, and the new understandings that will set the direction for the future of both Church and nation.

We can expect interest in our offerings in science, engineering, architecture, computer science and related fields. As the management of information becomes even more of a challenge than it is today, we can expect more enrollments in our School of Library and Information Science. Many students will come to prepare for careers in law, government, foreign service, business and organizational management. Many others will want the humanities, drawn by some inner impulse but unaware, perhaps, of just how much a technologically-driven society needs the humanization they will be able to provide. Philosophers and poets are needed as much as scientists and engineers to foster genuine progress in our national life. True to John Lancaster Spalding's founding vision, the University "will educate the minds that give direction to the age; it will be a nursery of ideas, a center of influence."

Music, drama, and the visual arts, particularly in their capacity to enrich society by fostering the creativity of the human spirit, will remain important parts of the mosaic that is The Catholic University of America. Similarly, the need for the provision of social services will equal the need for healthcare services in the century ahead; CUA's tradition of excellence in nursing and social work will be there in service to the future. So will our

Three thousand shades of color cover the surface of this mosaic of Christ that dominates the North Apse of the Shrine's Upper Church. The work by Polish immigrant John DeRosen covers 3,600 square feet and may be the world's largest mosaic of Christ.

capability to research the problems of youth, family, and an aging population, problems made all the more acute by the speed of technological change.

Most of our students over the past century have come here because the University is Catholic, because CUA is committed to the person and gospel of Jesus Christ as the primary source of values and attitudes reflected in the campus culture. Some students came for the specific purpose of gaining professional competence in one or another branch of religious studies and thus prepare themselves to contribute professionally to handing on the Catholic tradition. That will continue as even more young and not-so-young people will want preparation for pastoral and other forms of ordained and non-ordained ministry in the Church. The vast majority of students will continue to enroll here, however, to prepare themselves for secular pursuits. Why, then, will students continue to choose CUA?

Virtually all those who chose CUA in the past found here a real but undefined Catholic atmosphere, a recognition that education without God is incomplete. It is something more than simply living and studying "in the shadow of the Shrine," the great basilica built by the Catholics of America to honor Mary, the Mother of God, and constructed on land once owned by the University but now the property of The National Shrine of the Immaculate Conception, our closest neighbor and this area's architectural landmark. Attempts to articulate the Catholic atmosphere on campus invariably reduce to one word—"friendliness." A religious perspective on this would see "friendliness" as evidence of a theological virtue in our midst—a lived charity, coupled with community service, that has helped make the CUA campus different from many others for the past 100 years. Surely one of the outstanding differences at this institution is its willingness to commit itself, as a University, to chartered service to the Church through the work of its ecclesiastical faculties in theology, philosophy, and canon law. But a pervasive characteristic, Church-related though not Catholic in any proprietary or exclusionary sense, is simply the friendliness of the place. Part of the optimism that propels us into our second century is the hope that the characteristic charity of CUA will open up new stages of growth for community on campus and for the nation and Church this campus is committed to serve.

"Lamp of Learning, Light of Faith," says it all rather well. The photographs of Fred Maroon—all 109 of them—say it even better. This reflection need not run on. It can end here with full confidence in the potential of a picture to serve as substitute for and enlargement of mere words.

Before the pictures pick up the story, however, one last written word is necessary, a word of praise and thanks to God for the gift of faith and the vocation, given to thousands, to live the life of the mind in the faith-committed community that is The Catholic University of America.

William J. Byron, s.j., is President of the University

The day is gone when you can deprive our brainy, ambitious young women from the highest and best education. She insists in having all the advantages of her brother, and she is right. The world "do move."

Sister M. Euphrasia, S.N.D.
Nov. 9, 1898, letter to
Rector Thomas J. Conaty

Pages 22-23. A statue of Mary, Queen of Students, graces the front of Gibbons Hall, a collegiate Gothic-style building, dedicated in 1911 to honor the first chancellor, Cardinal James Gibbons, archbishop of Baltimore. Clare Fontanini, former head of the art department, created the statue.

Pages 24-25. The late afternoon sun accents the architectural and sculptural features of the west entrance of the Shrine, site of many University liturgical celebrations. The desire of the University's fourth rector, Bishop Thomas Shahan, to build a suitable University church led to the proposal that the National Shrine be constructed next to campus as an expression of the American people's devotion to Mary.

Left. The Rev. Robert Paul Mohan, professor emeritus of philosophy, has taught social and political philosophy for more than 40 years. A popular undergraduate teacher, he is also an outstanding homilist.

Above. Caught up in Father Mohan's philosophy lecture is Katherine Teeling, an English major from Sayville, N.Y. Philosophy remains a cornerstone of the core curriculum.

Pages 28-29. Students "catch some rays" on Pryzbyla Plaza, named for benefactor Edward J. Pryzbyla, a 1925 graduate and native of Chicopee, Mass.

Pages 30-31. When snow falls in Washington, the spacious mall between Gibbons and McMahon halls becomes a favorite gridiron for touch football players.

Left. Student nurses listen to a chemistry lecture by Assistant Professor Diane Bunce in the auditorium of Maloney Hall. Below. Back row: Rosemary McConnell of Washington Township, N.J. Center row: Jill E. Wisgirda of Brockton, Mass., and Tanya L. Nolle of Silver Spring, Md. Front row: Rhodora Marie Donahue of Pittsburgh, and Maureen Ridder of New Rochelle, N.Y.

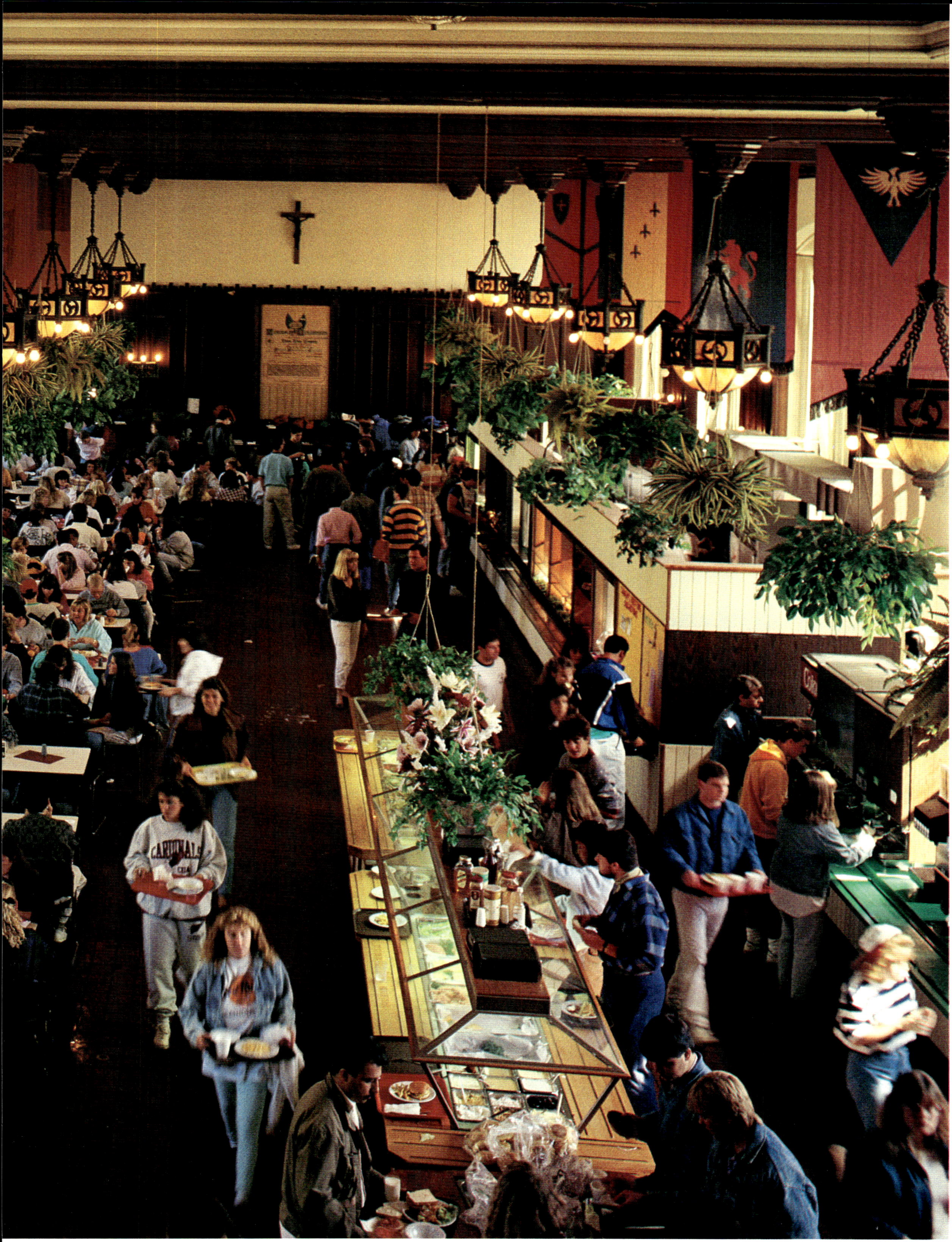
CARDINALS

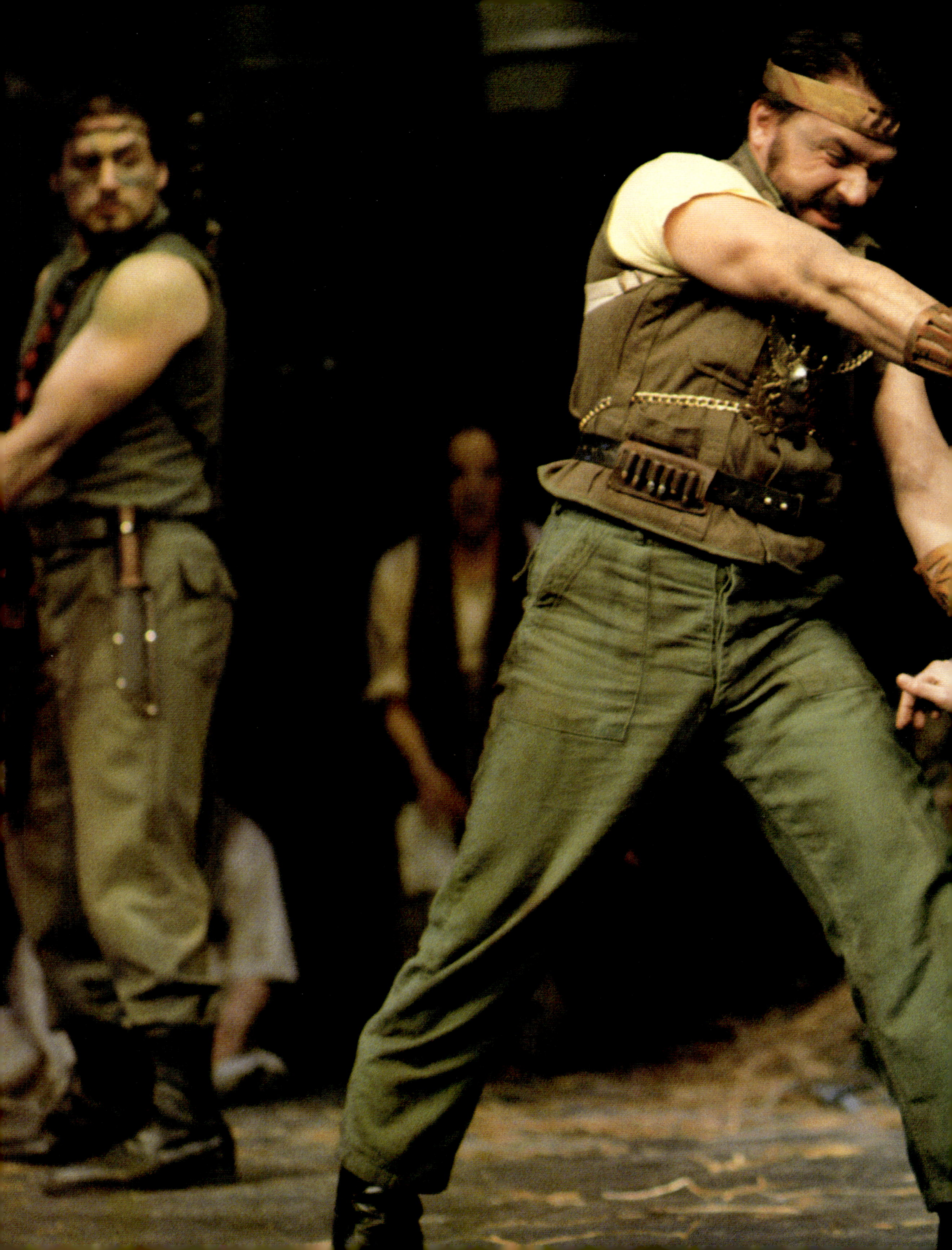

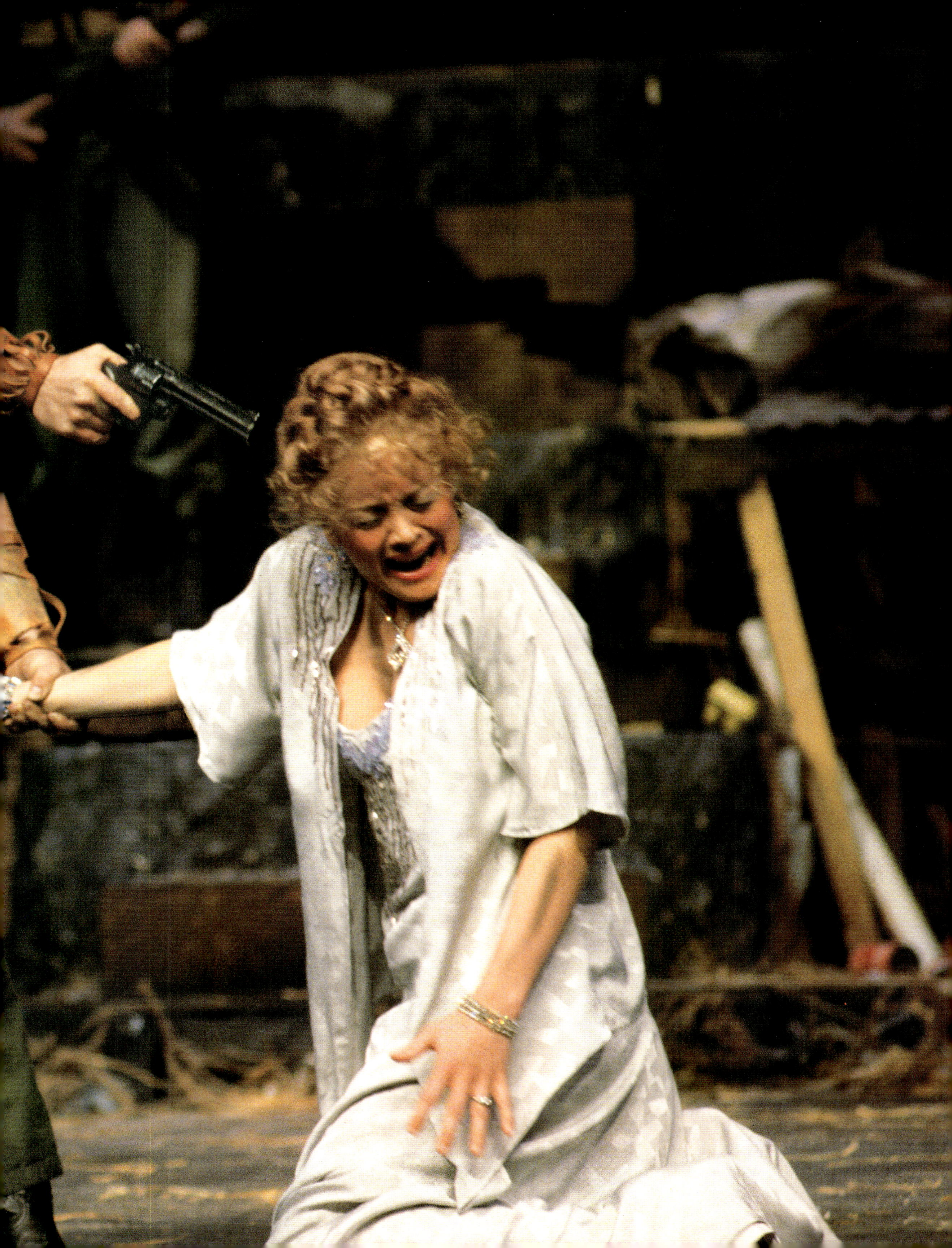

... We were called up on stage by Father Hartke ... We gathered and waited, and then Father said quite gently and quietly, "We're going to have a few moments of prayer." Well, that was something new for this old trouper. And it had a phenomenal effect. Gone were the nerves. Gone were the butterflies in the stomach. Gone were the terrors of what might go wrong. Strength flowed in. And ever after that, I have prayed before an opening night.

Helen Hayes
recalling her 1964 CUA residency in the
title role *Good Morning, Miss Dove,*
and her 1971 return to play
Long Day's Journey Into Night.

Pages 34-35. University Center Dining Hall in University Center West is a popular lunchtime meeting place that accommodates about 600 students. The building opened in 1914 as Graduate Hall and housed the University's first Knights of Columbus Fellows.

Pages 36-37. Graduate drama students Robert J. Napoli of Aliquippa, Pa., and Pamela Martin of Lancaster, Pa., perform a crucial scene in Hartke Theatre's production of *The Trojan Women.* Founded more than 50 years ago, the drama department combines training in the theater arts with a liberal arts education.

Right. "Broadway Night" is a popular annual production held in Hartke Theatre by the Benjamin T. Rome School of Music. Named for its major benefactor, a 1934 architecture alumnus and trustee emeritus, the music school is a cultural asset that offers the Washington metropolitan area more than 300 performances a year.

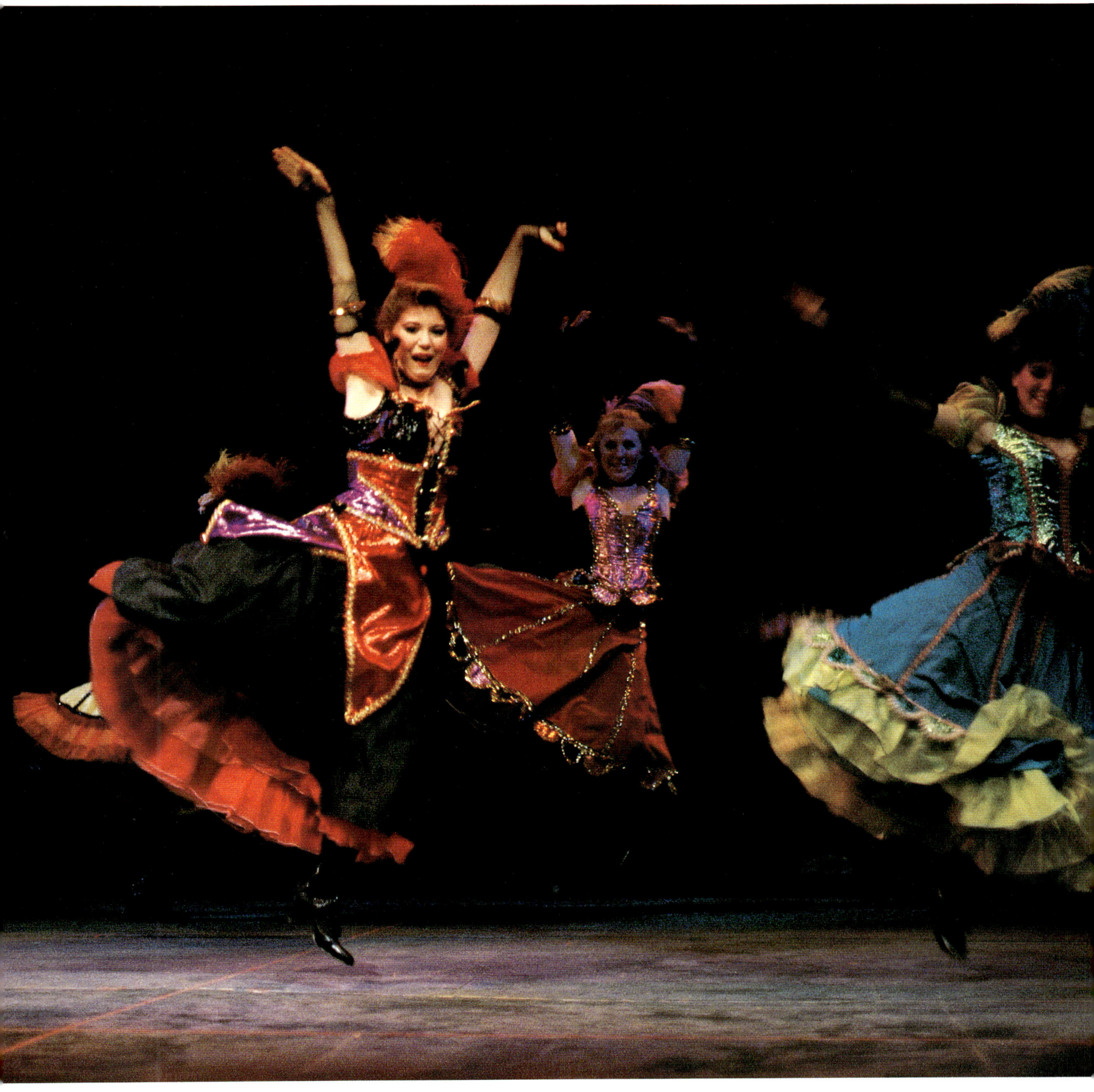

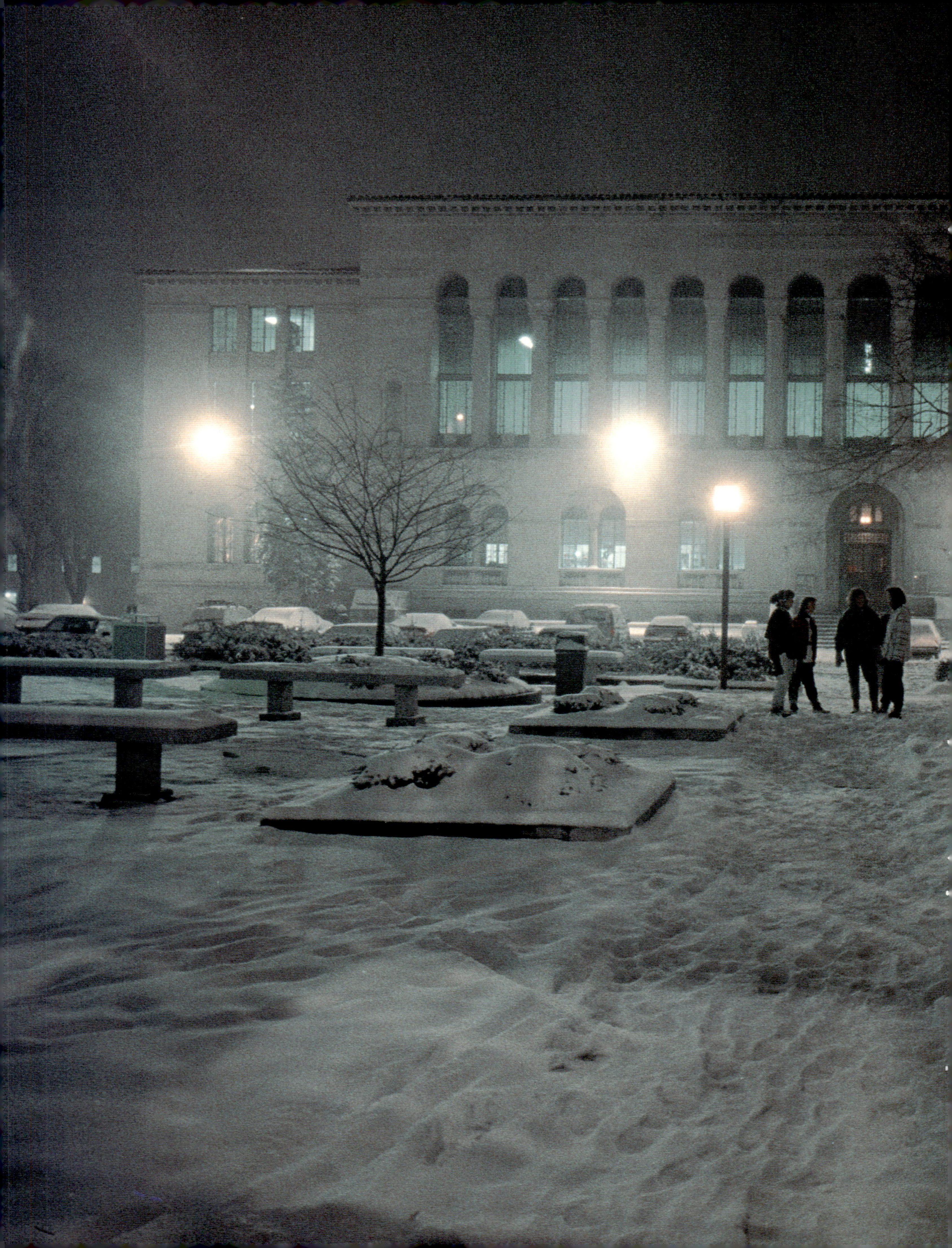

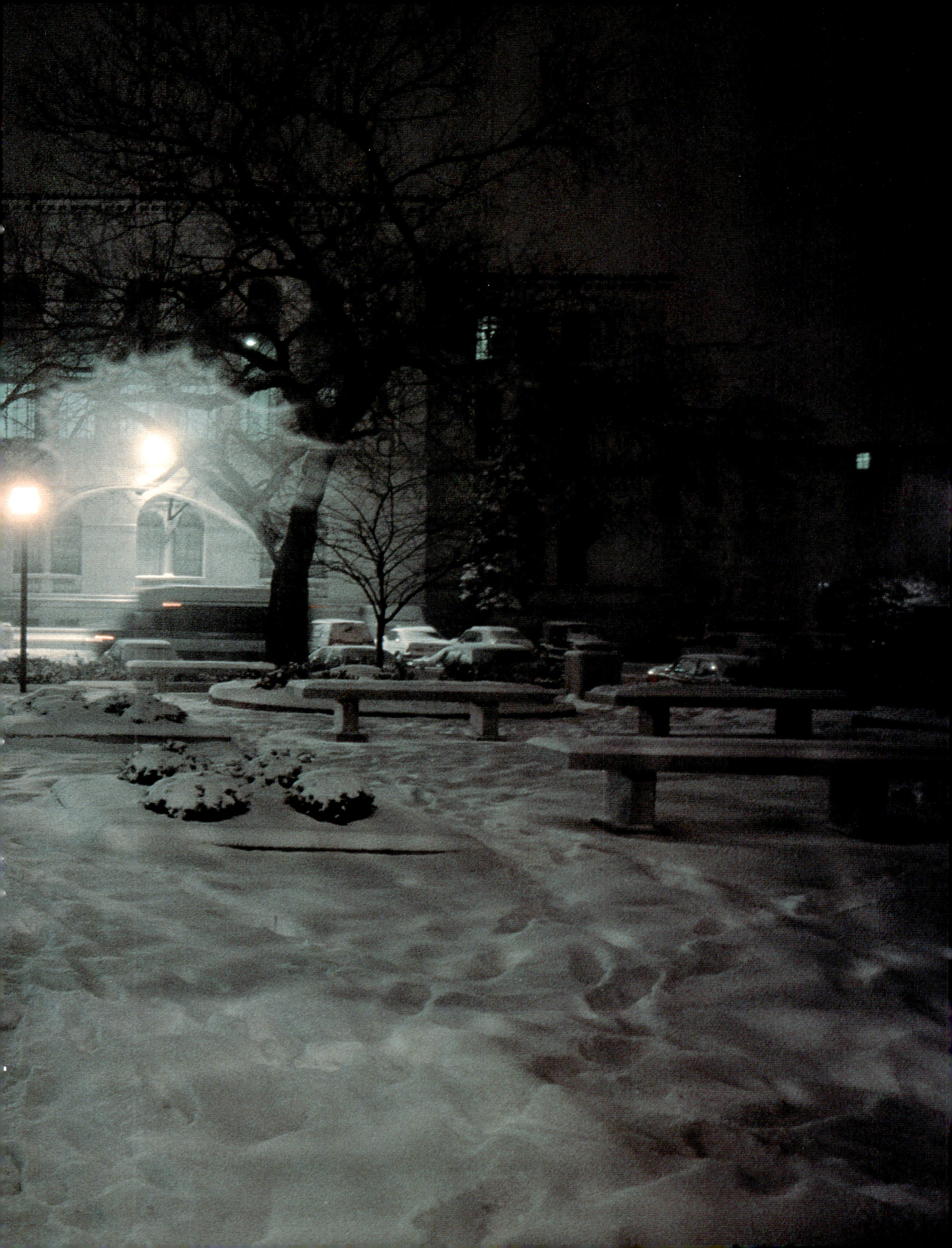

Pages 40-41. Lights from the John K. Mullen of Denver Memorial Library brighten the winter campus at night. The building houses more than one million volumes and honors the Denver milling and mining magnate.

42

Enjoy the privileges of your youth: the right to be dynamic, creative and spontaneous; the right to be full of hope and joy; the opportunity to explore the marvelous world of science and knowledge; and above all the chance to give of yourself to others in generous and joyful service.

Pope John Paul II
Oct. 7, 1979
visit to campus

Above. "The Alarm" rock group entertains students at a concert at the Raymond A. DuFour Athletic Center.

Right. Julie Wrobel, a French major from Boston and Sarah White, an English major from Summit, N.J., keep fit with aerobics classes offered by the athletic department at the Raymond A. DuFour Athletic Center. The center's other amenities include an indoor jogging track, dance studio, swimming pool, racquetball and squash courts, and saunas.

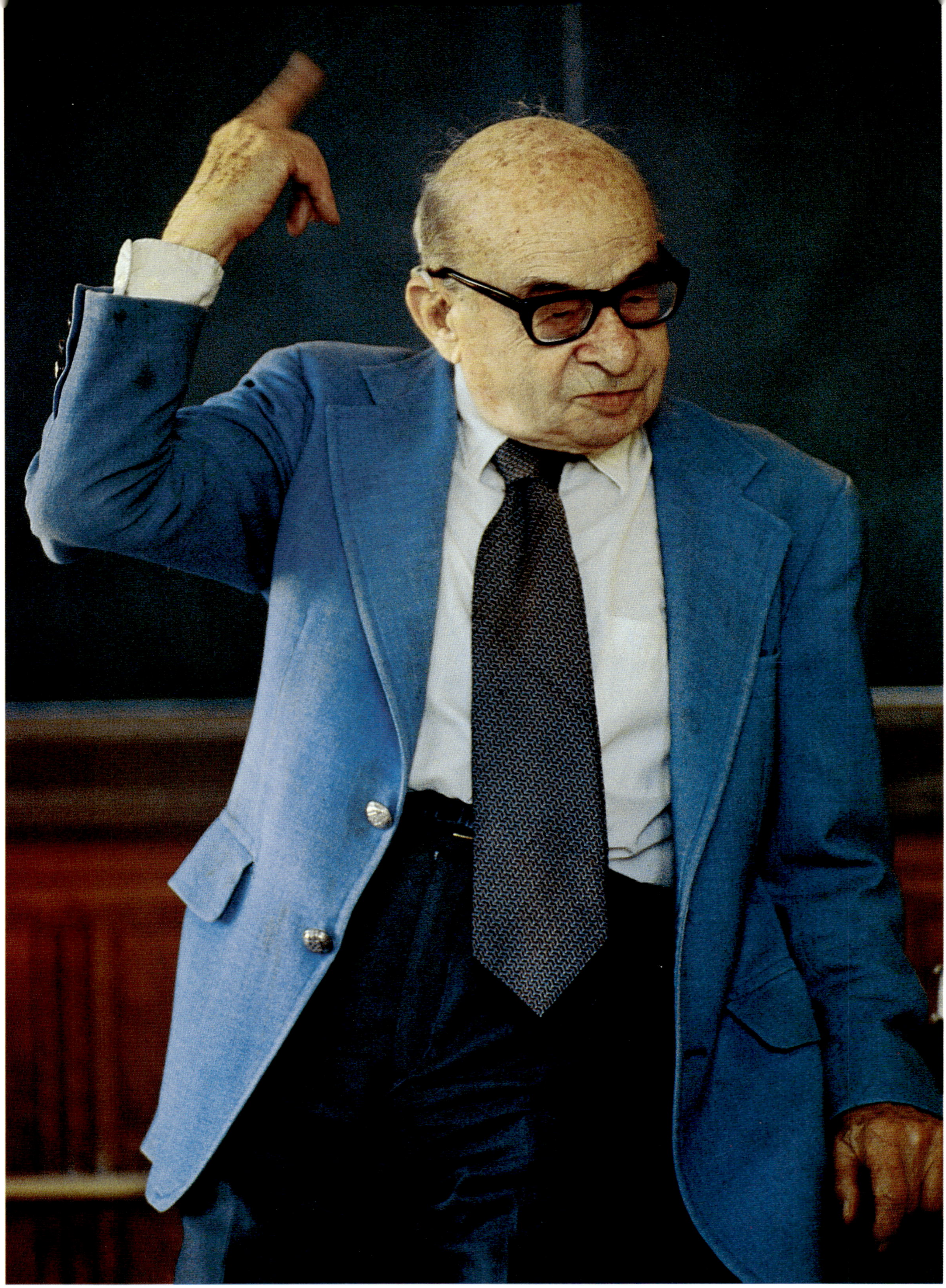

This country needs a university center of Catholic thought, where religion and science in their highest forms may combine to make known the marvelous truth of God. Its mission should be to unify and elevate it to set a definite standard of scholarship that will arouse in clergy and laity a love for the highest intellectual attainments. Thank God this has been done by Catholic University.

Bishop Thomas J. Conaty
Dec. 8, 1902, banquet for
Apostolic Delegate Diomede Falconio

Left. Paul Weiss, the Heffer Professor of Philosophy, drives home a point during class. He teaches full time in the School of Philosophy, which celebrates its centennial in 1995. In peer evaluations, the School of Philosophy ranks among the foremost in the nation.

Right. Listening intently to a philosophy lecture are, center, economics and business majors Matthew Burns of Cheshire, Conn., and Gregory Mortenson of Birmingham, Ala.

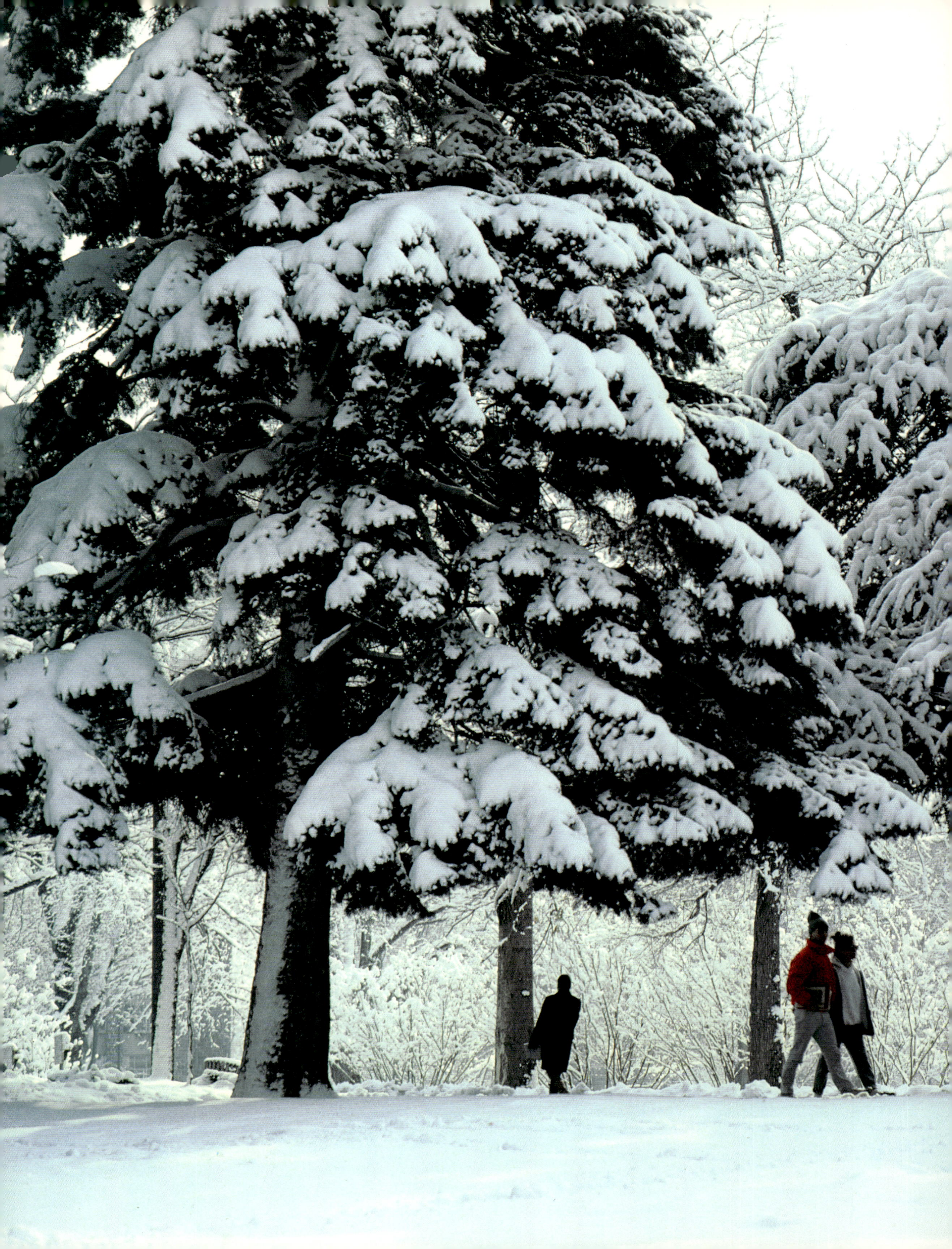

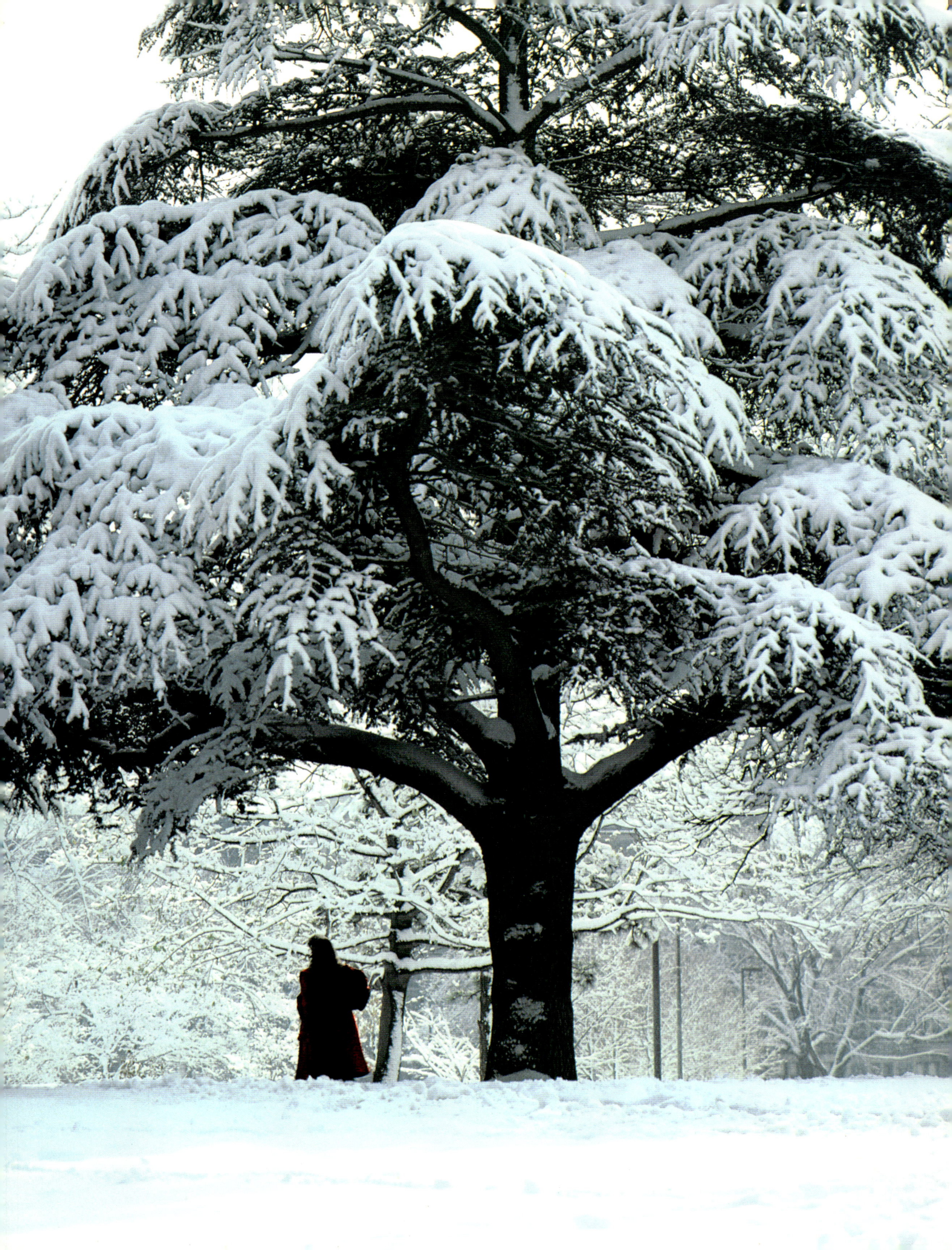

Pages 46-47. Heavily laden with snow, branches swoop to form a canopy for students walking to classes at this unique University—the national University of the Catholic Church and the nation's only University established by the bishops of the United States.

Above. The John F. Kennedy Center for the Performing Arts' Concert Hall provides the setting for a scholarship benefit concert by CUA's School of Music, the only music school to hold an annual concert at the center.

Right. John Benskin of Washington, D.C., a doctoral candidate in music composition, perfects his viola technique in the University Symphony Orchestra. CUA music students have opportunities to study with professors who are first-chair players with organizations such as the National Symphony Orchestra in Washington.

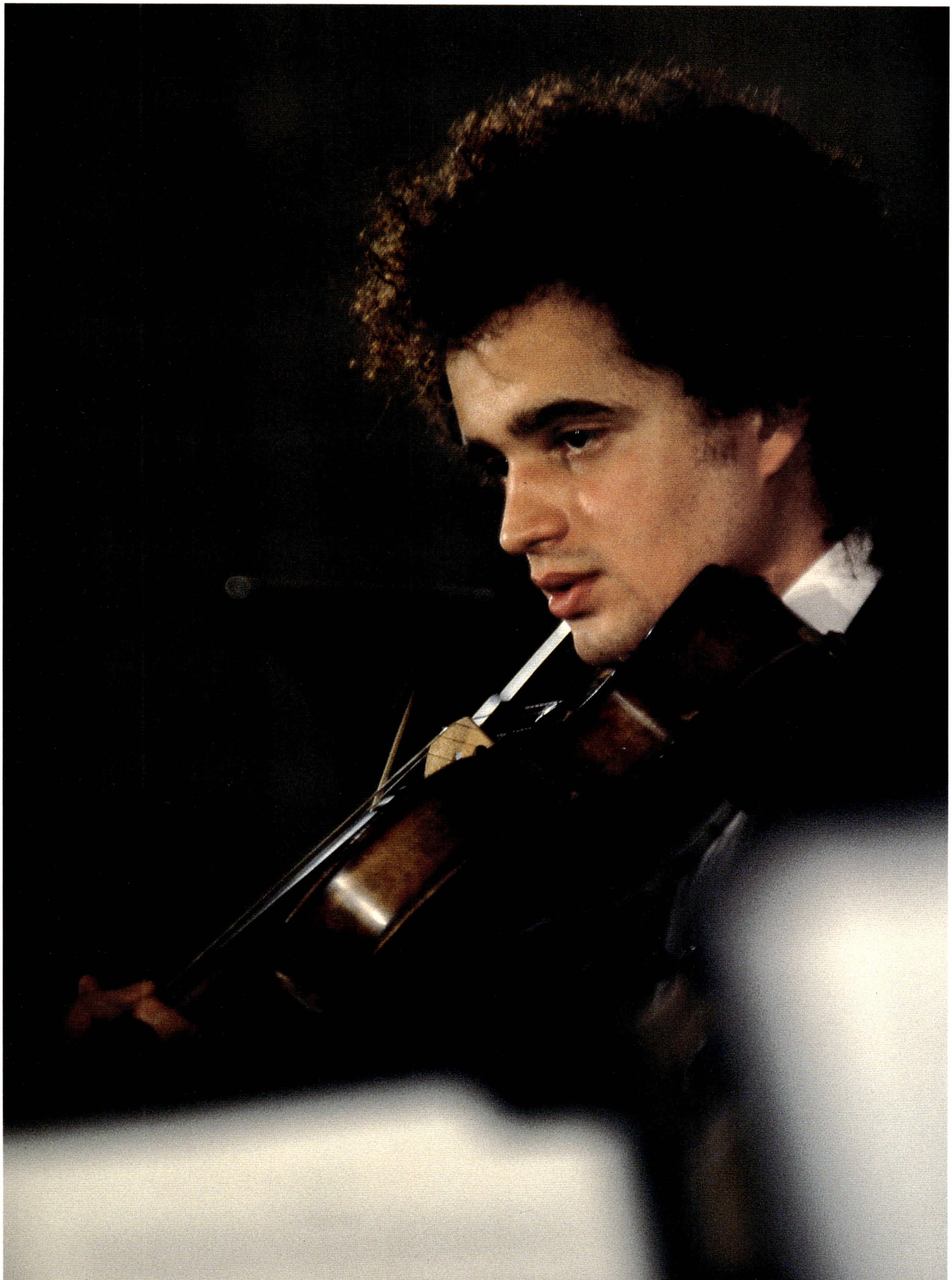

I am often asked if my architecture training has influenced my photography, and of course it has. Architecture studies, in addition to providing a professional degree, offered a great liberal arts education.

Fred J. Maroon
Century Ended, Century Begun
1990

Left. From detailed drawings to scale models, ideas by architects take shape. For his cultural intervention studio project, Tom Krizmanic of Monona, Wis., designs a proposal for a historic district in Nimes, France.

Below. Architecture students got a home of their own when the "Old Gym" became the sparkling Edward M. Crough Center for Architectural Studies, named for the 1950 civil engineering alumnus.

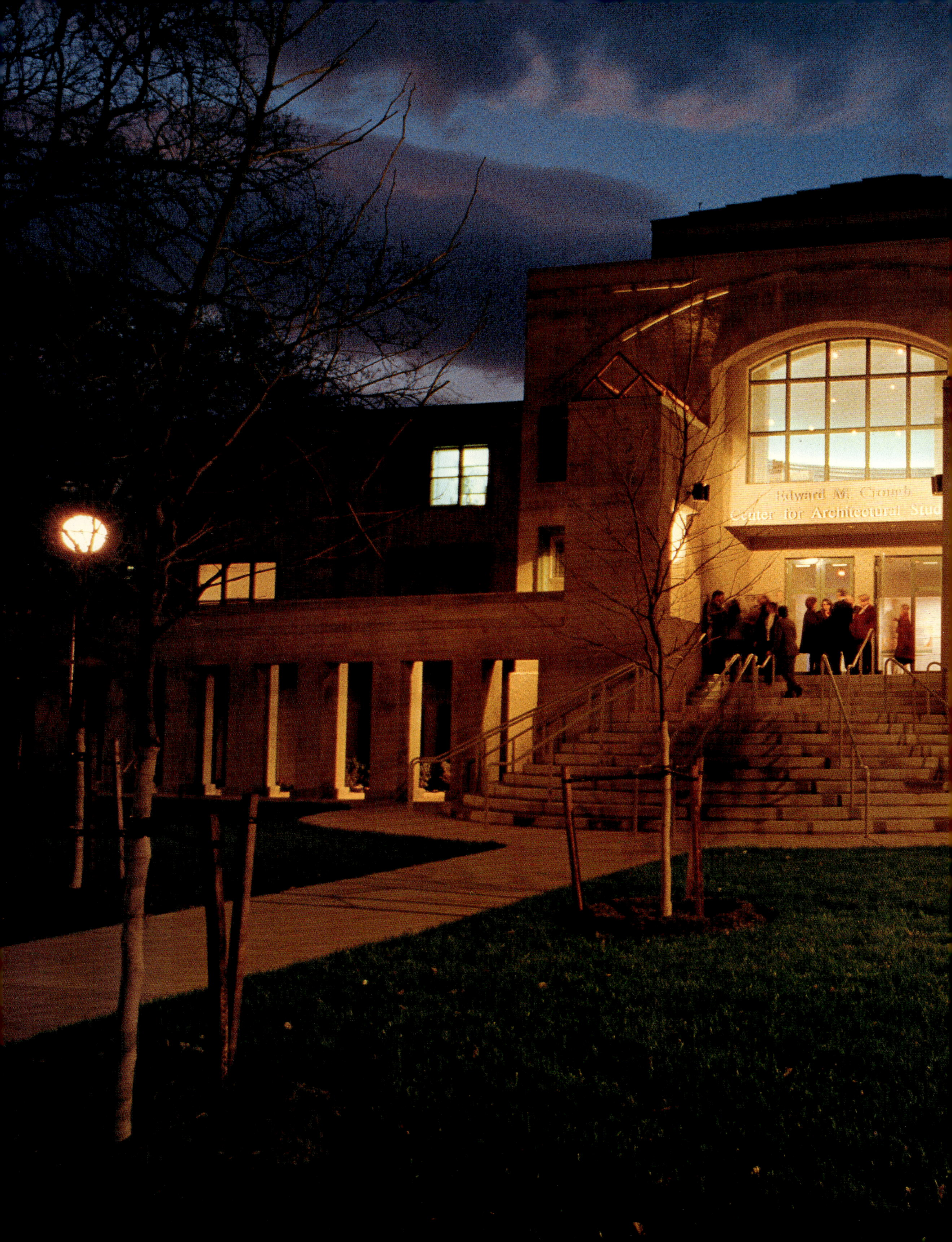
Edward M. Clough
Center for Architectural

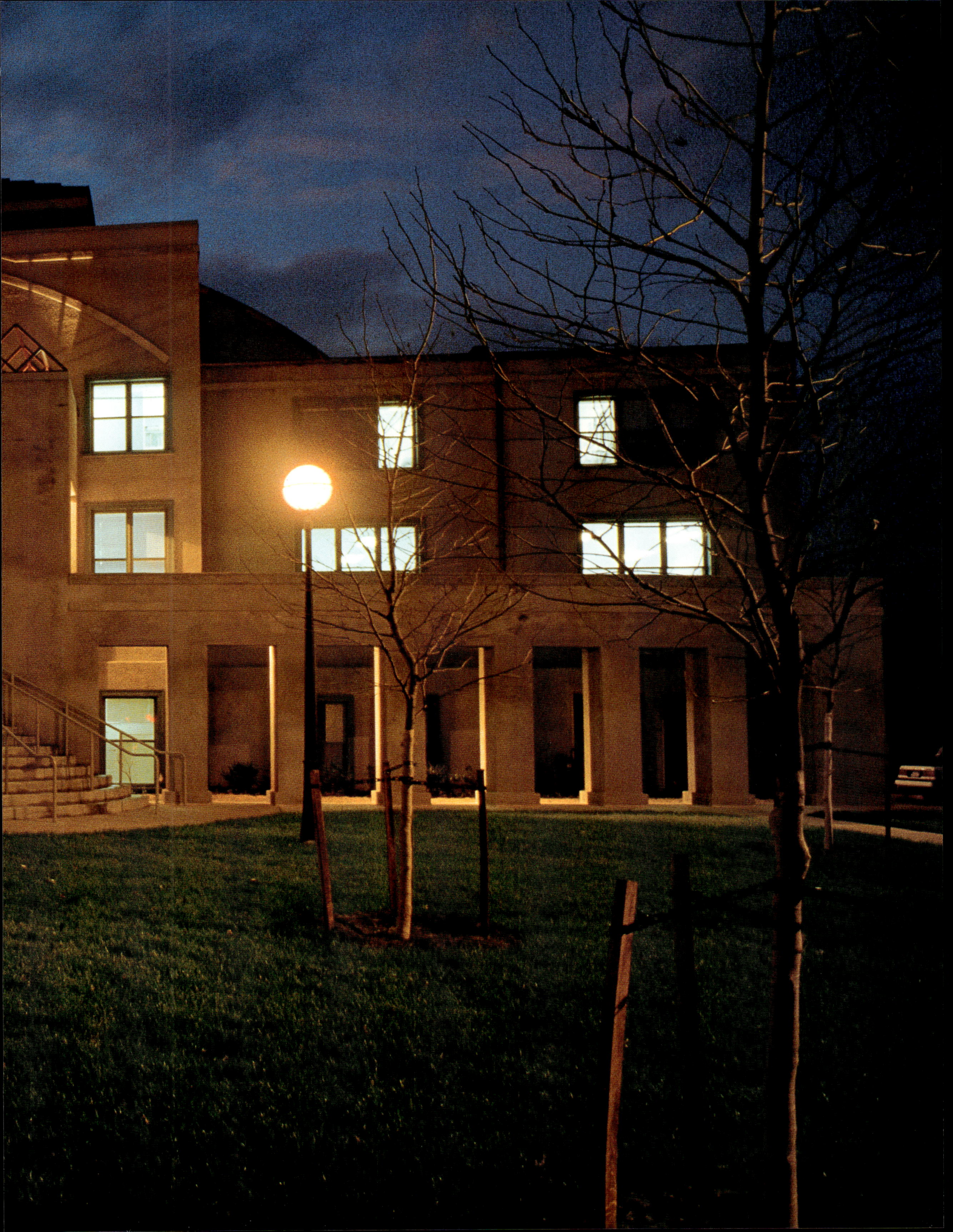

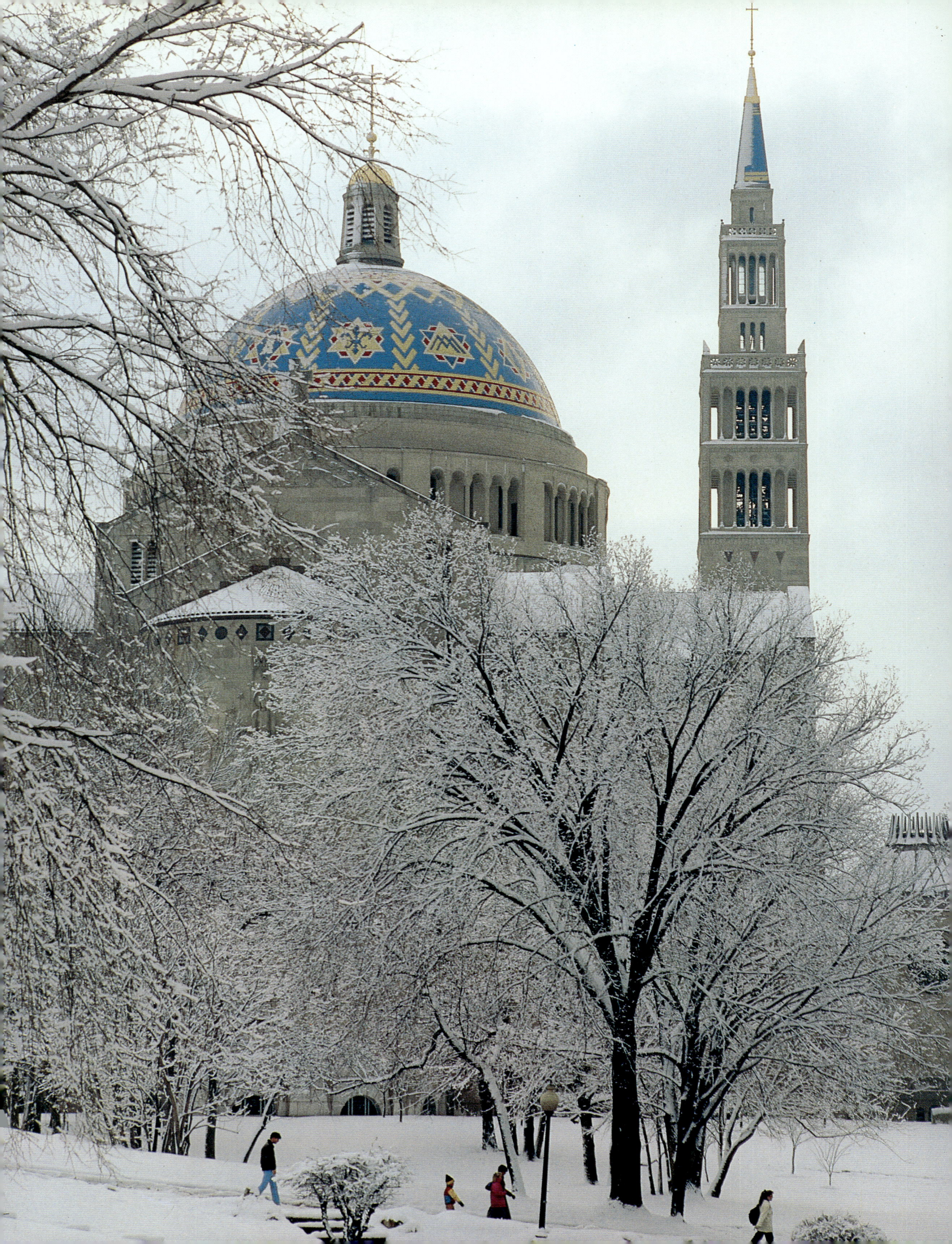

Pages 52-53. Twilight gives the Edward M. Crough Center for Architectural Studies a chance to show another side of its resplendent luster.

Left. The gold, blue and red dome of the Shrine and the Knights' Tower, with 56 carillon bells, rise from the snowy blanket covering the campus. Former University Trustee John McShain built the Upper Church and regarded it as the "greatest project" he ever undertook. Cardinal Patrick O'Boyle, former archbishop of Washington and University chancellor, guided the Upper Church's construction.

Above. The rose window above the Shrine's main entrance features gold and amethyst accents associated with Byzantine architecture. Unlike rose windows in Gothic architecture, the Shrine's windows are in a wheel pattern with heavy stone spokes radiating from the center.

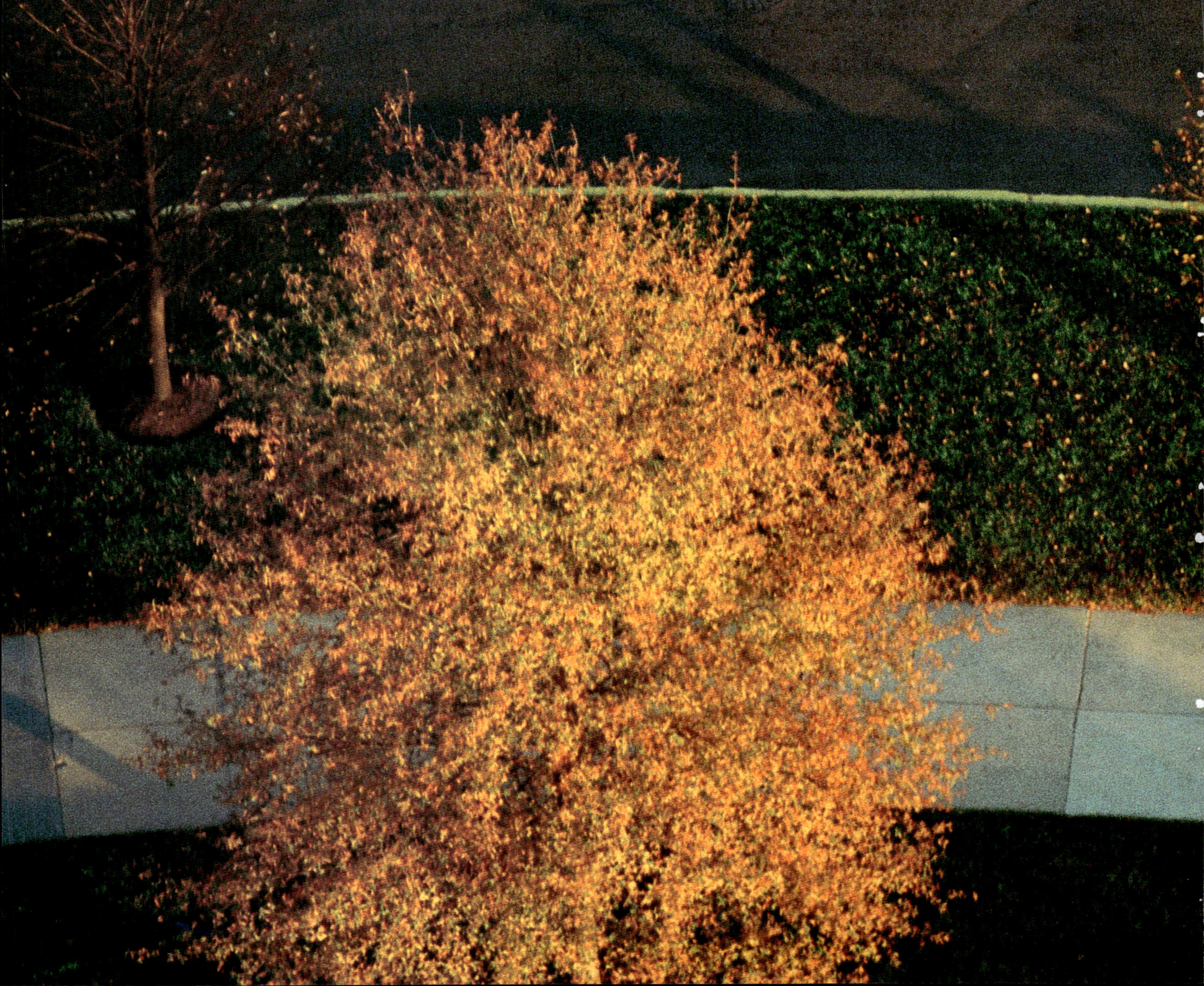

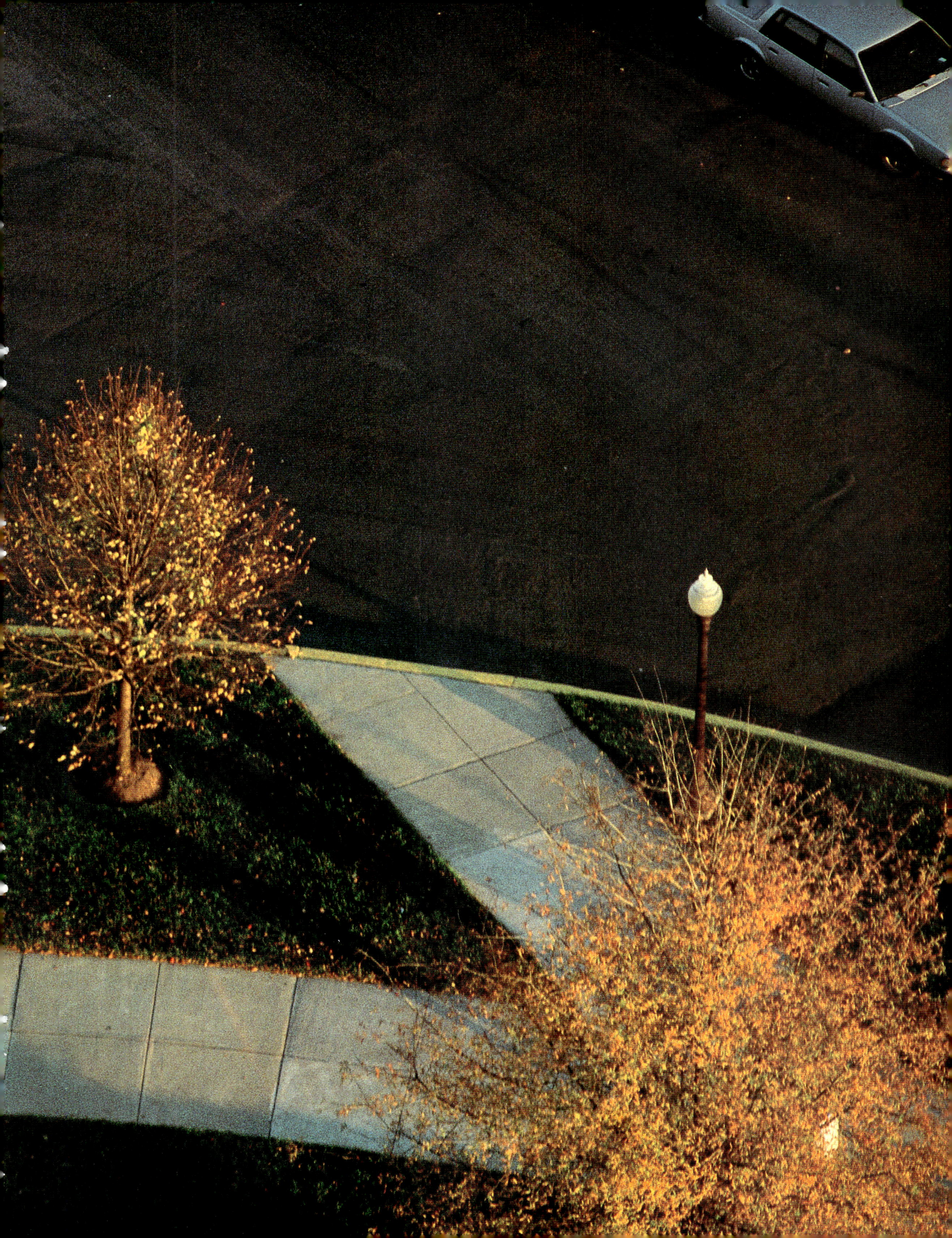

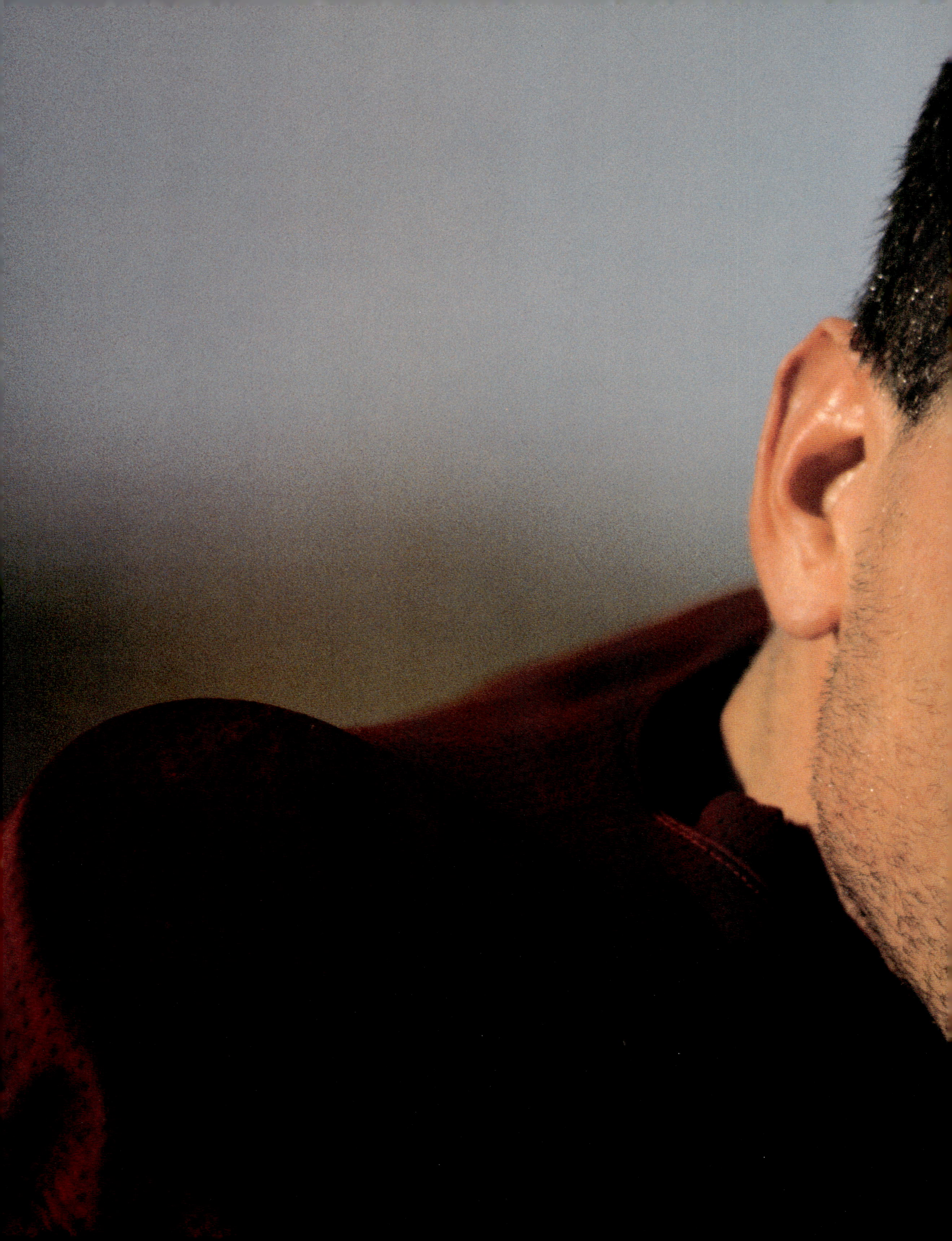

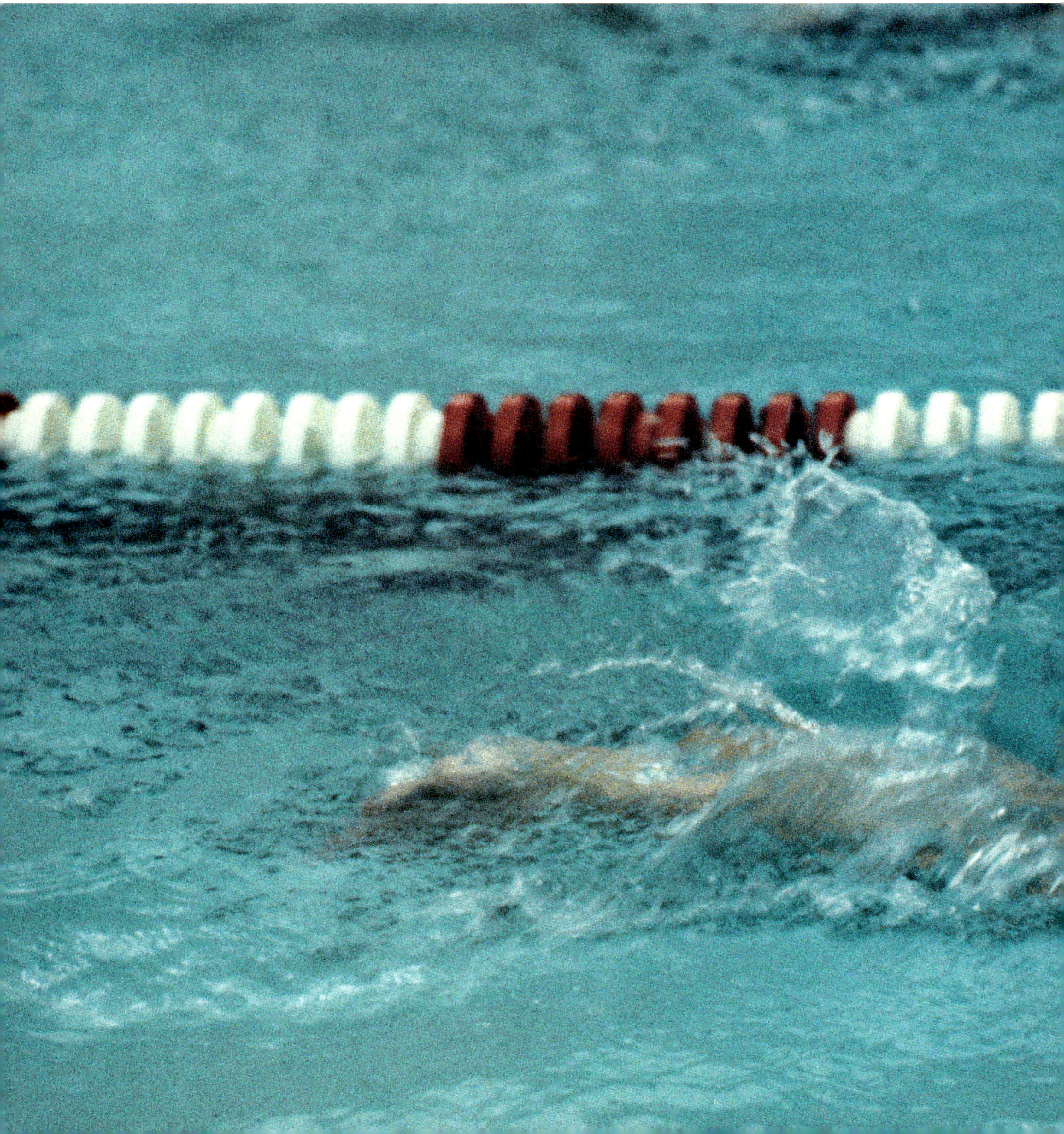

Say, this is some place.

President Theodore Roosevelt
during an impromptu campus visit in 1905

Pages 56-57. Cyclists whiz past golden-leafed trees that dot the campus in autumn.

Pages 58-59. Fighting Cardinal quarterback Drew Komlo of College Park, Md., readies for battle on the field at the Raymond A. DuFour Athletic Center. The 40-acre complex is named for a benefactor from the class of 1928, trustee emeritus and former football star.

Above. School of Nursing major Kellie Dunphy of Maple Glen, Pa., and University mascot, alias Joan Carlin, of Ardsley, N.Y., help rouse CUA football fans.

Right. President William J. Byron, S.J., joins Homecoming King Sean D. Mahaney of Akron, Ohio, and Queen Lourdes M. Casares of Coral Gables, Fla., psychology majors, on the sidelines to watch the Homecoming football game.

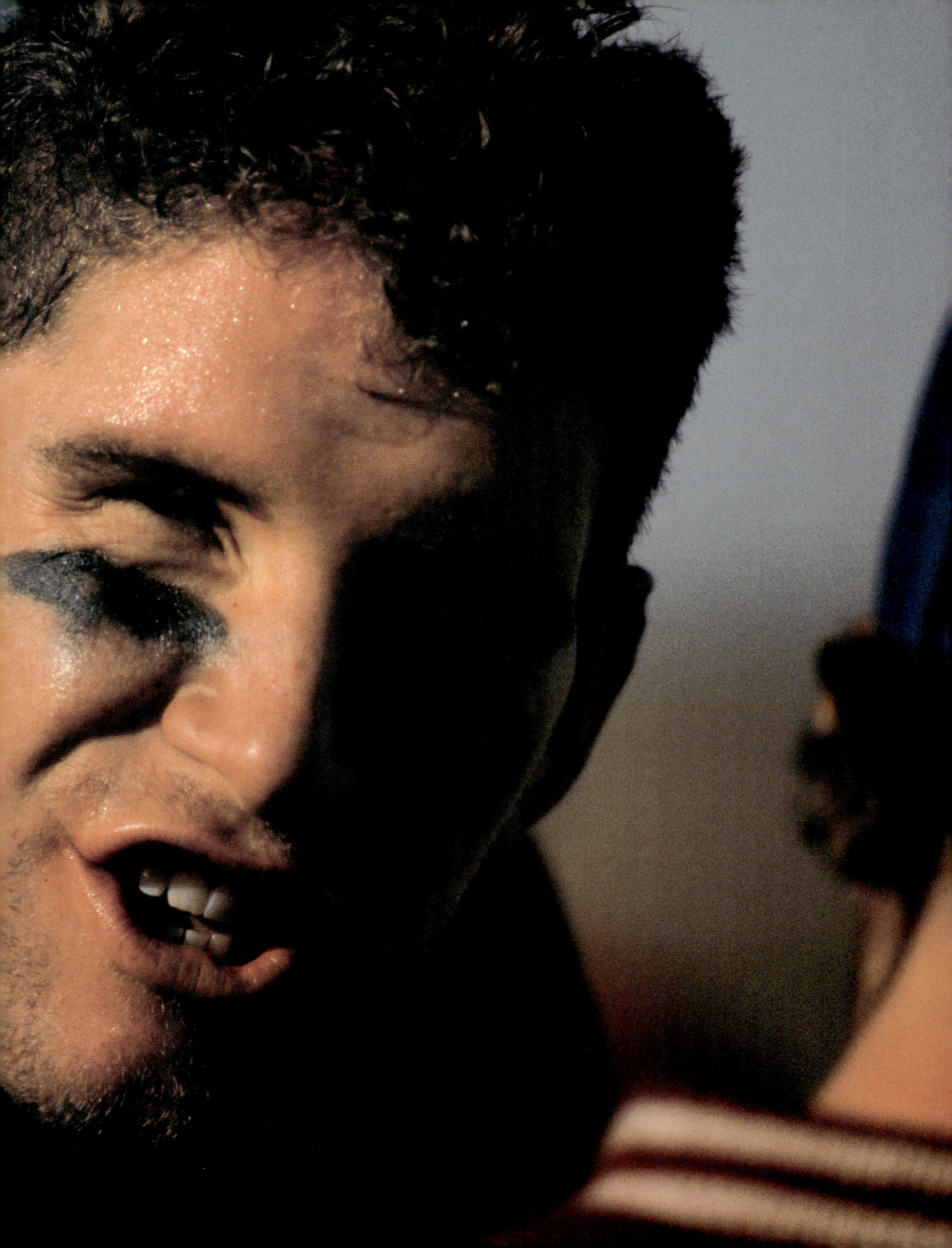

A member of the women's swim team competes at the athletic center's pool. CUA's women swimmers matched their male counterparts' success by winning nine meets without a loss during the 1989-90 season.

While studying literary theory, methodology and criticism at CUA, I began to realize the extent to which music encodes values, history and faith of my people.

Sister Thea Bowman, F.S.P.A.
M.A. '69, Ph.D. '72

Left. No matter what instrument a musician plays, talent, discipline, practice and proper techniques are essential. Distinguishing the music school is strong academic and professional training taught by a dedicated faculty in Washington, where opportunities abound.

Right. Music programs advance toward perfection in Ward Hall, built in 1934 and named after Justine Bayard Ward, whose estate endows liturgical music studies.

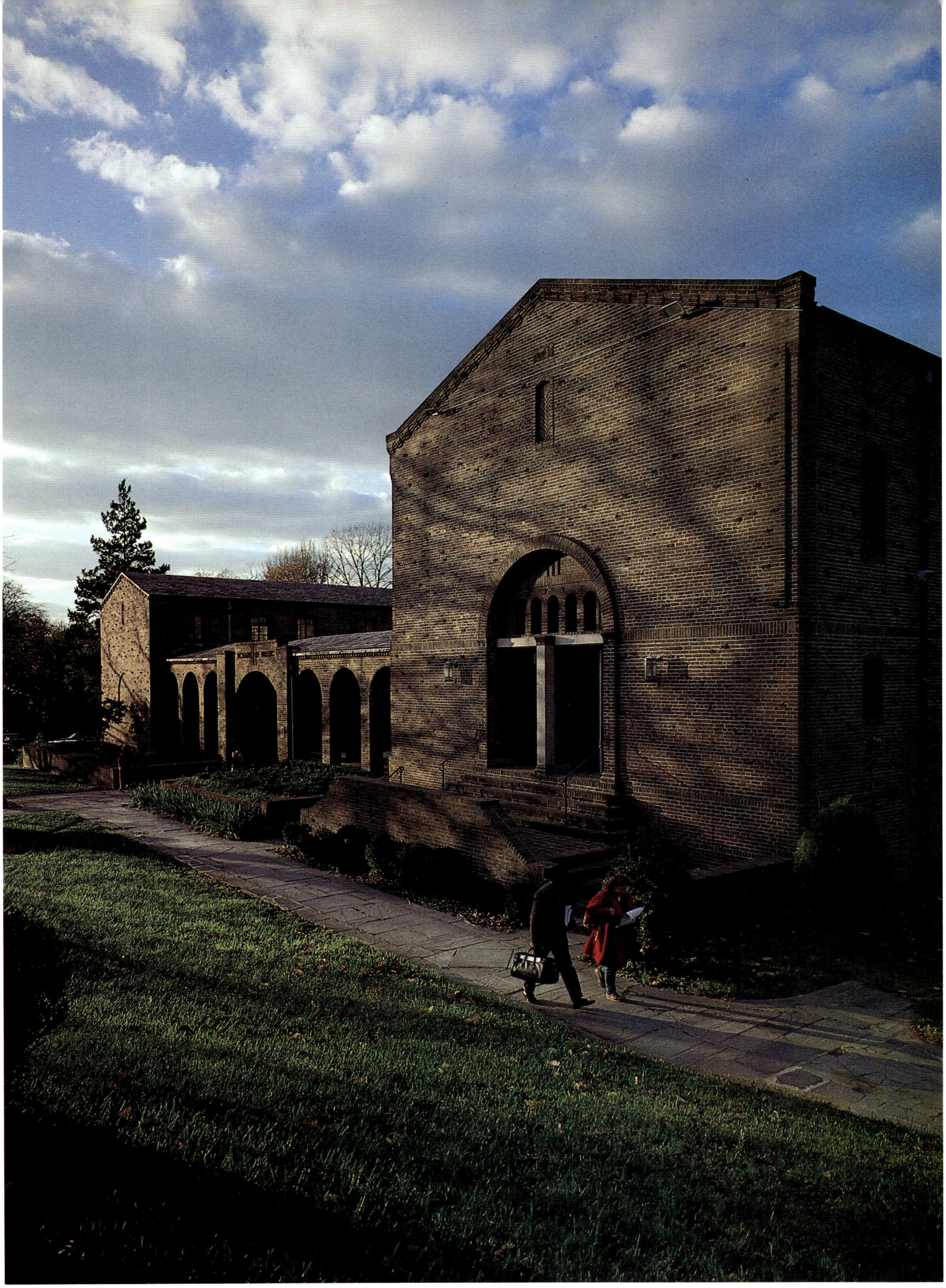

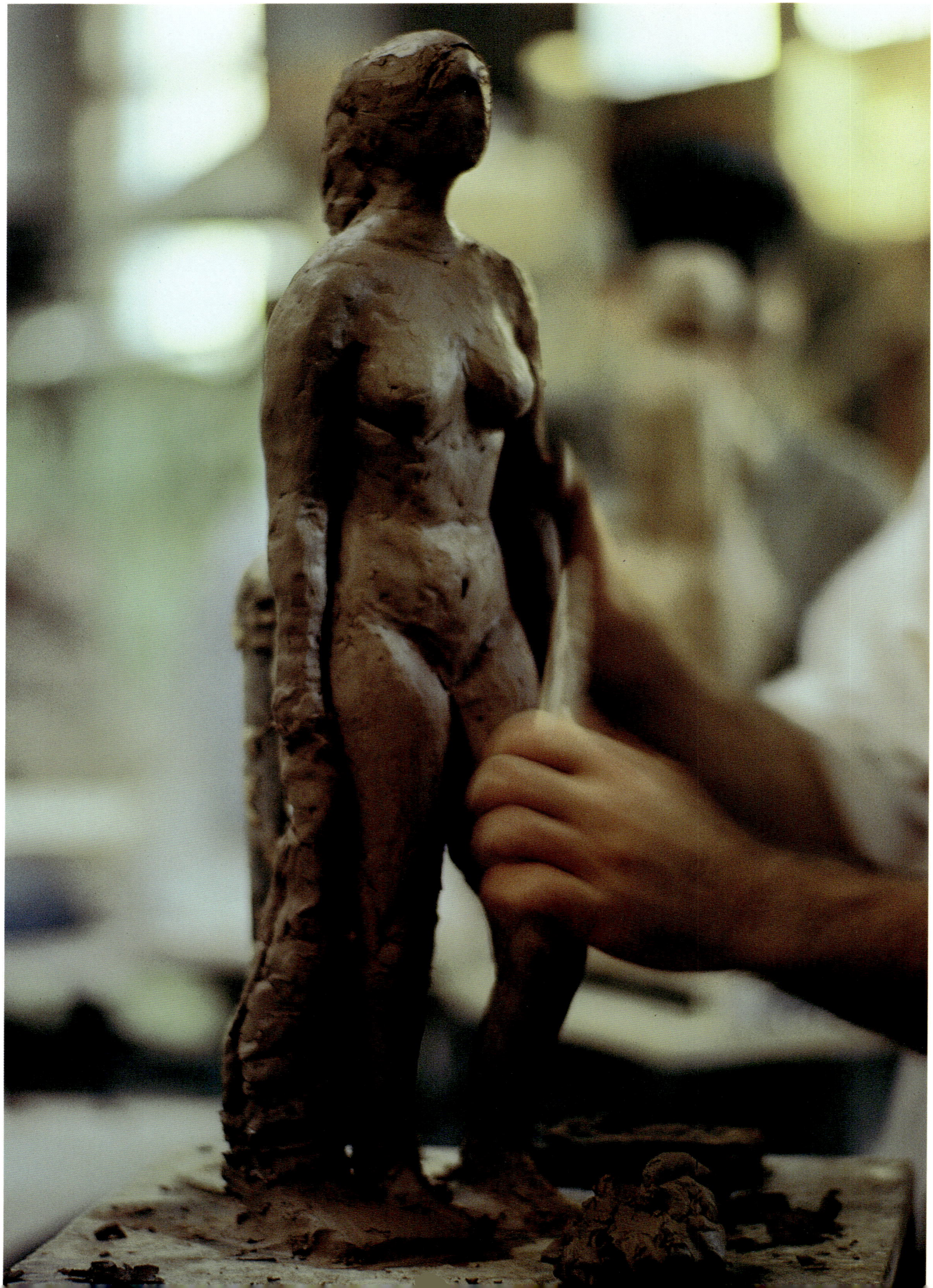

To paint is the most wonderful thing in the world. Not to paint is one of the worst.

Andrea de Zerega
Painting Instructor
Art Department
1948

Left. A sculptor puts the finishing touches on a clay model.

Above. Jeffrey Kim, a history major from Beckley, W.Va., and Kathryn Caputo of South Orange, N.J., take advantage of opportunities for non-art majors to put brush to canvas.

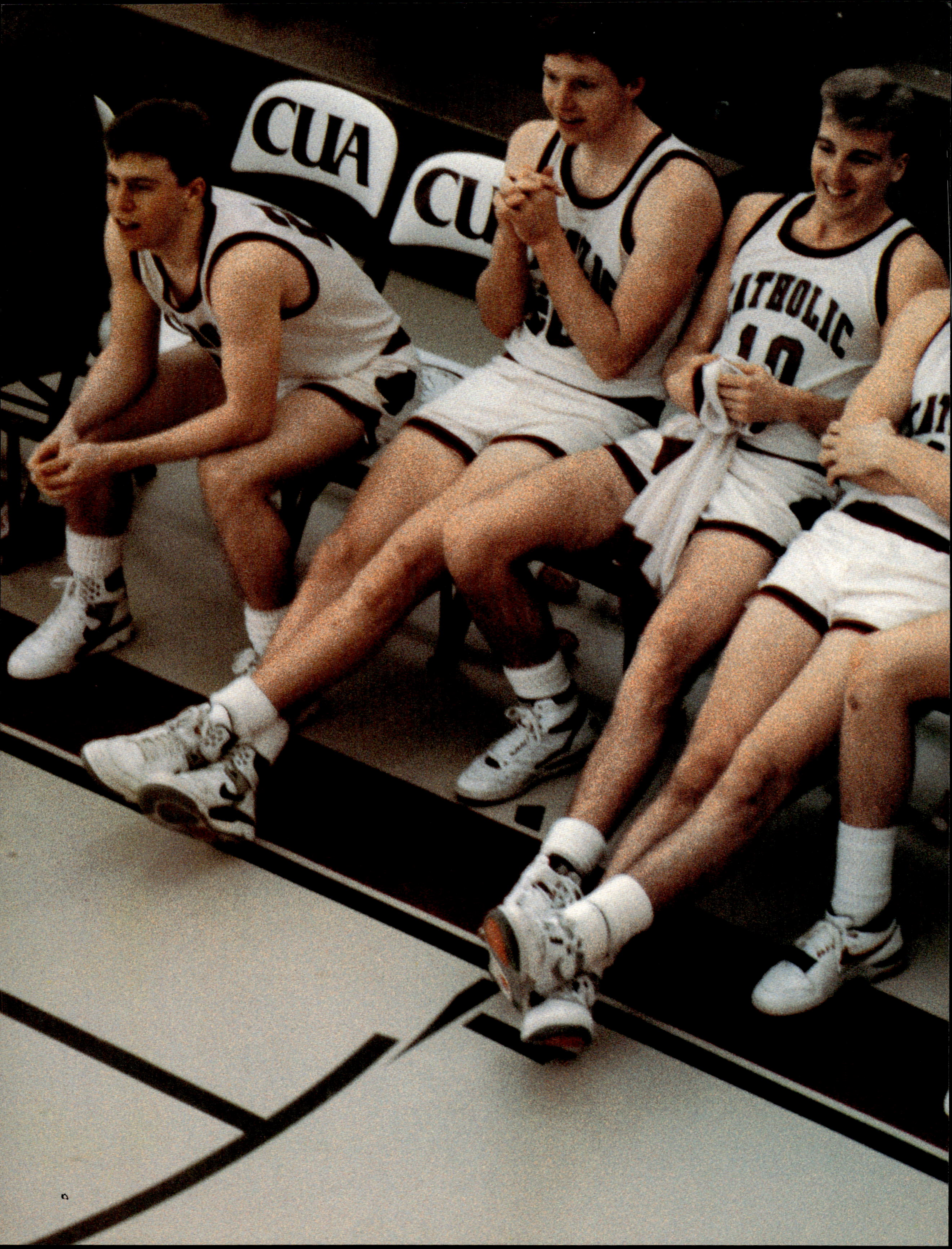
CUA
CATHOLIC
10

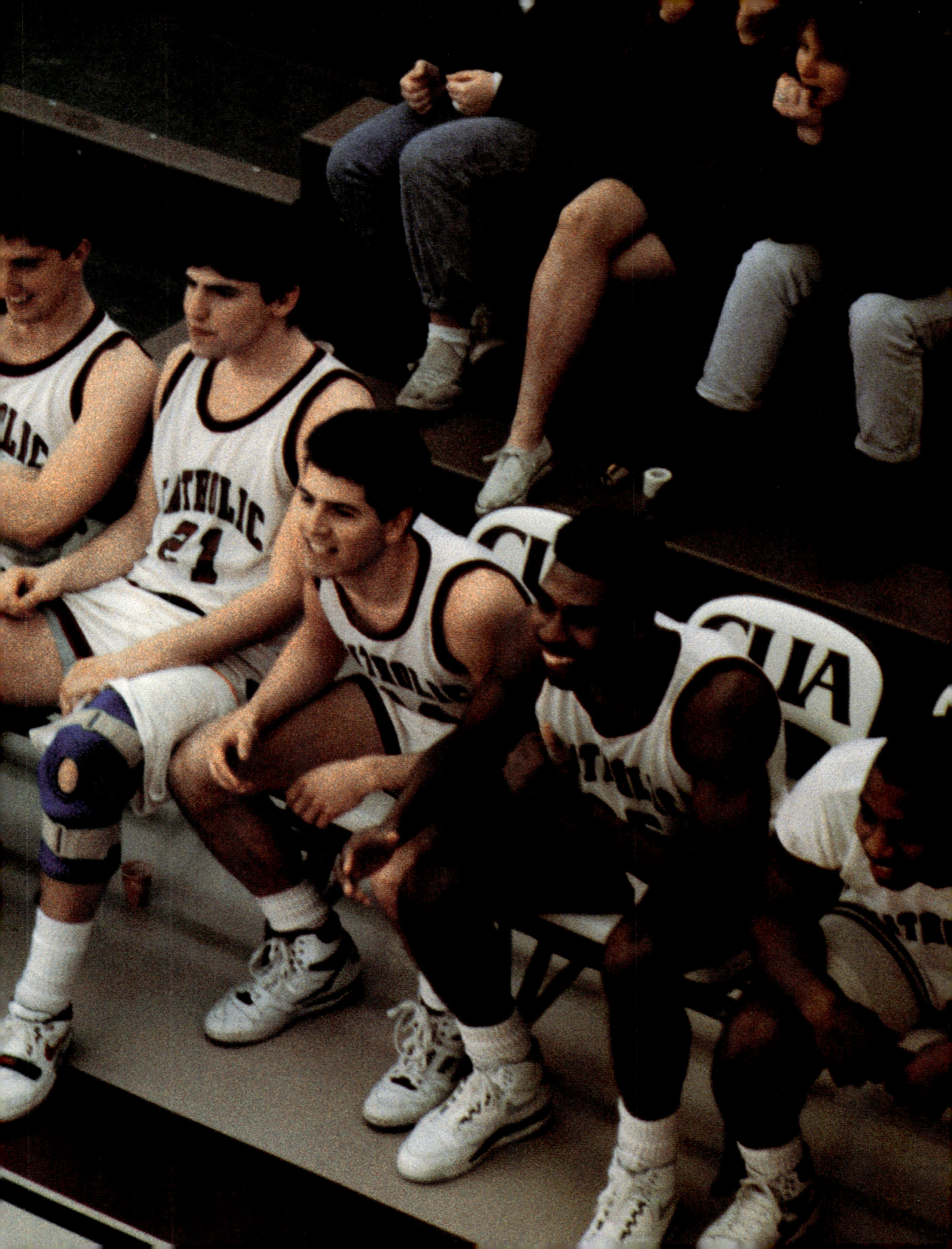
21

Pages 68-69. Cardinal basketball players share a light moment during tough Division III competition.

You . . . have received through the gift of faith and the special gift of this University a role in making America's future.

Cardinal Terence Cooke of New York
Homecoming 1979

Above. On the board in a calculus class is a formula for finding the volume of a wedge of wood cut from a tree. Daniel Gallo, associate chairman of the Department of Mathematics, explains the equation.

Craig A. Jones, a biology major from Hyattsville, Md., works on a physics project in Hannan Hall. The building's 1987 dedication culminated the dream started by Karl F. Herzfeld, internationally known physicist and former physics department chairman.

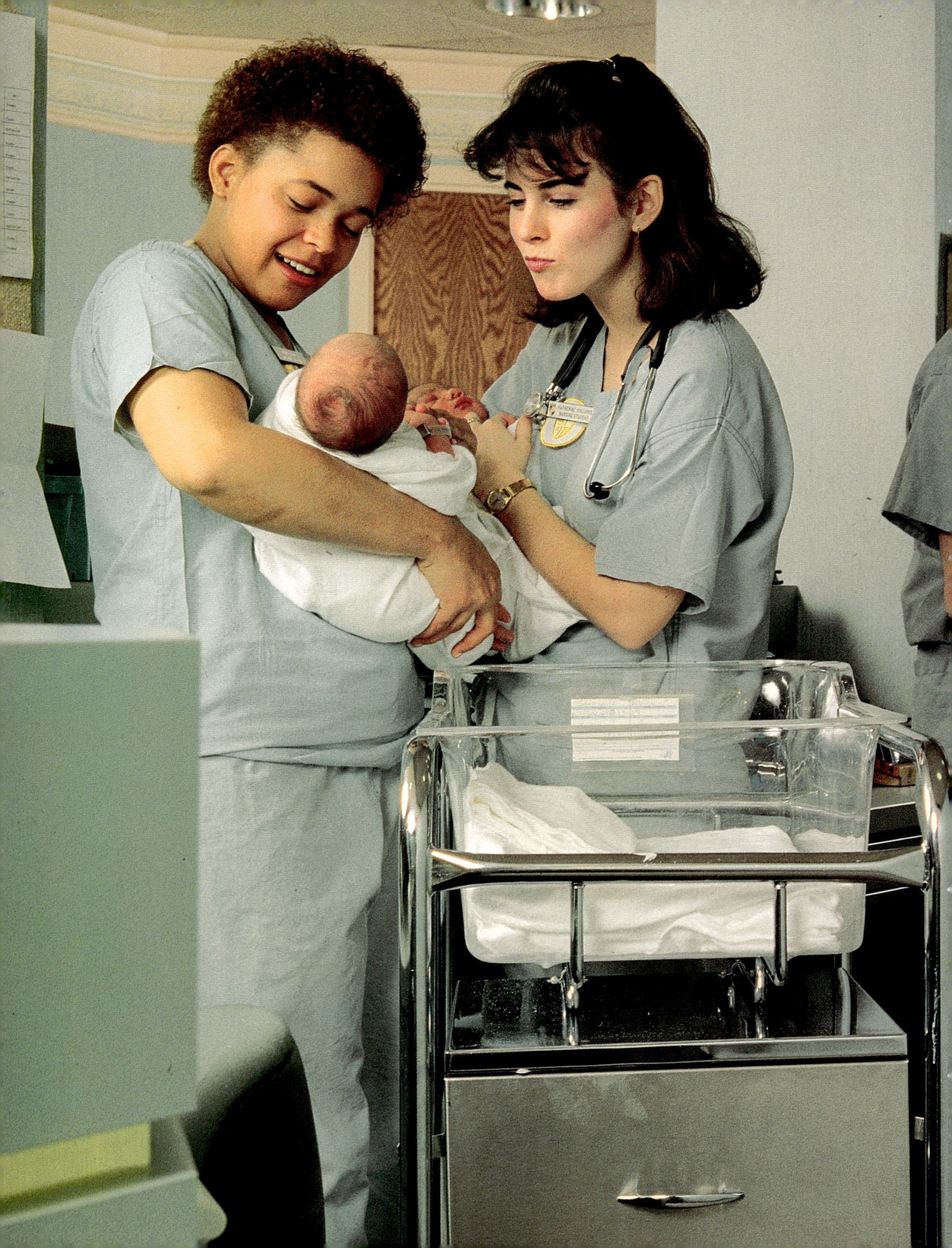

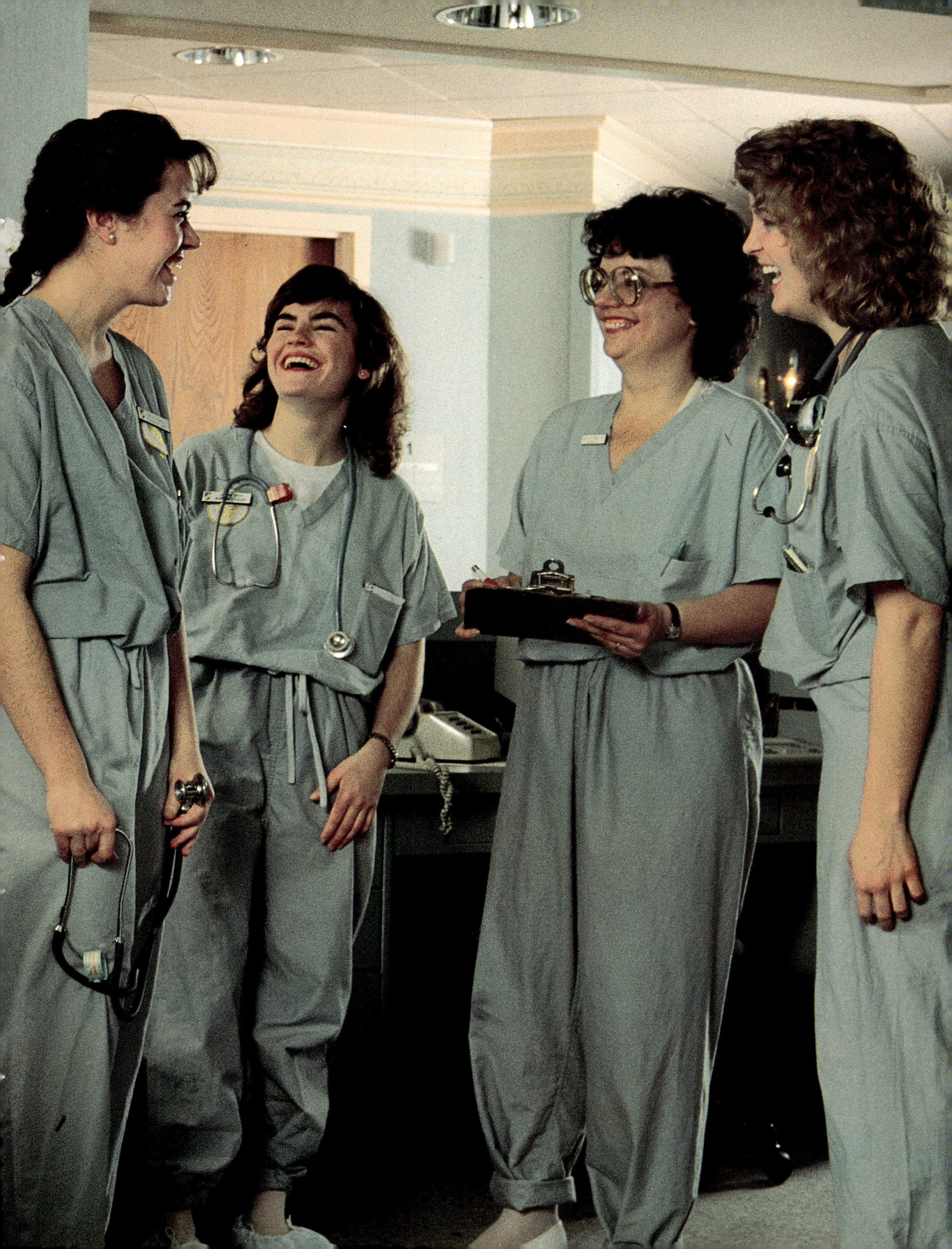

We therefore most gladly welcome and heartily approve your project for the erection of a university, moved as you are by a desire to promote the welfare of all and the interests of your illustrious Republic . . . having laid the foundations of an institute destined to provide the Church with worthy ministers for the salvation of souls and the propagation of religion, and to give the Republic her best citizens.

Pope Leo XIII
April 10, 1887,
letter approving
CUA's establishment

Pages 72-73. School of Nursing students prepare for professional practice by working in clinical settings at Providence Hospital and other major medical centers and hospitals.

Left. A young violinist perfects her technique at the Washington Suzuki Institute, a week of concentrated instruction held every summer at the music school.

Right. String players follow the call of spring by taking to a wooded glade to capture the intricacies of Mozart. Making up this trio are Christopher J. Shenkel of Hyattsville, Md.; Karen A. Clark of Hopewell Junction, N.Y.; and Jonathan R. Jones of Fort Washington, Md. Music students provide music services to churches, embassies, agencies and hospitals.

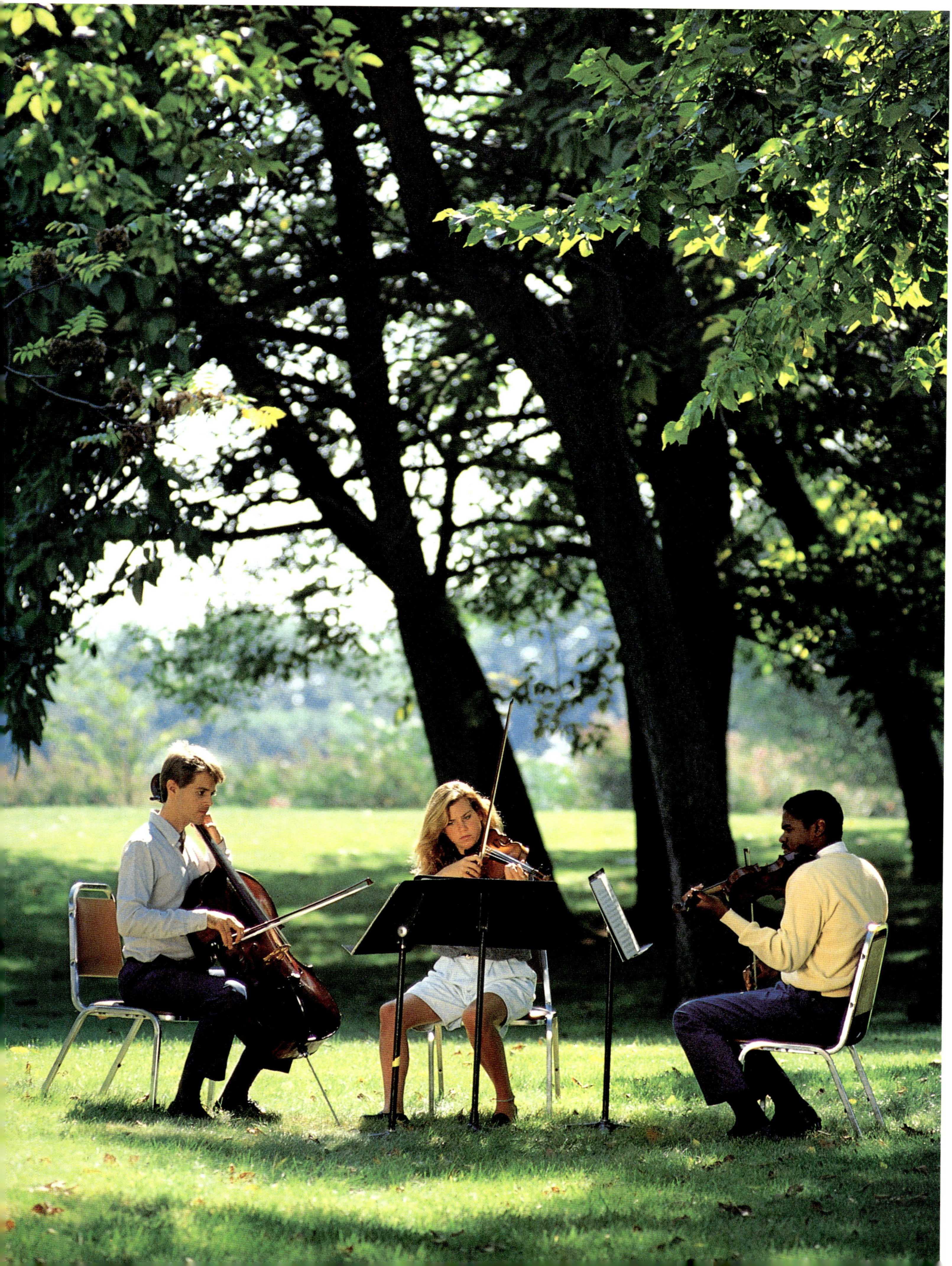

COLLEGE
BOSTON
BILL MURRAY
Budweiser
Come to Bacardi
With a Touch of Comfort.
LEAVE COLLEGE WITH A LASTING IMPRESSION.
NO GUTS. NO GLORY.

The Catholic University of America is a national treasure that has served both the nation and Church well for a century. . . . Every Catholic in the country can be proud of it.

Lee Iacocca
Chairman and CEO
The Chrysler Corporation
April 10, 1987
Centennial Dinner

Enjoying a few moments of relaxation in Centennial Village's McDonald House are 1990 class members James A. Montaldo of Succasunna, N.J., Soren C. Hulgaard of Rye, N.Y., and Paul R. Dougherty of Potomac, Md., son of Dean Jude Dougherty of the School of Philosophy.

Below. Robert Destro, associate professor of law, guides students through fine points of the Constitution.

Right. A favorite campus meeting place is the steps of stately McMahon Hall, which opened in 1895 to honor Monsignor James McMahon, a New York pastor and benefactor.

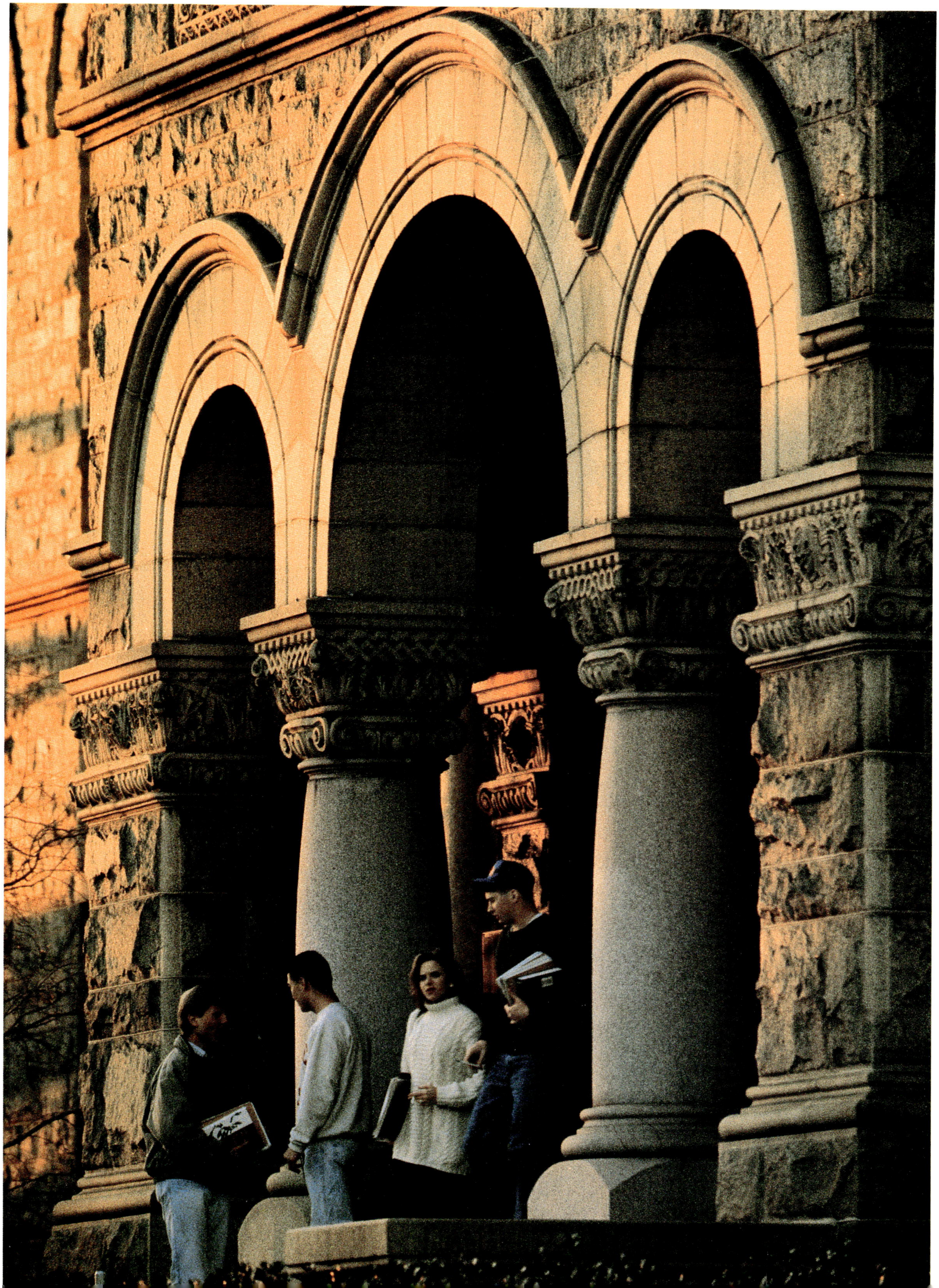

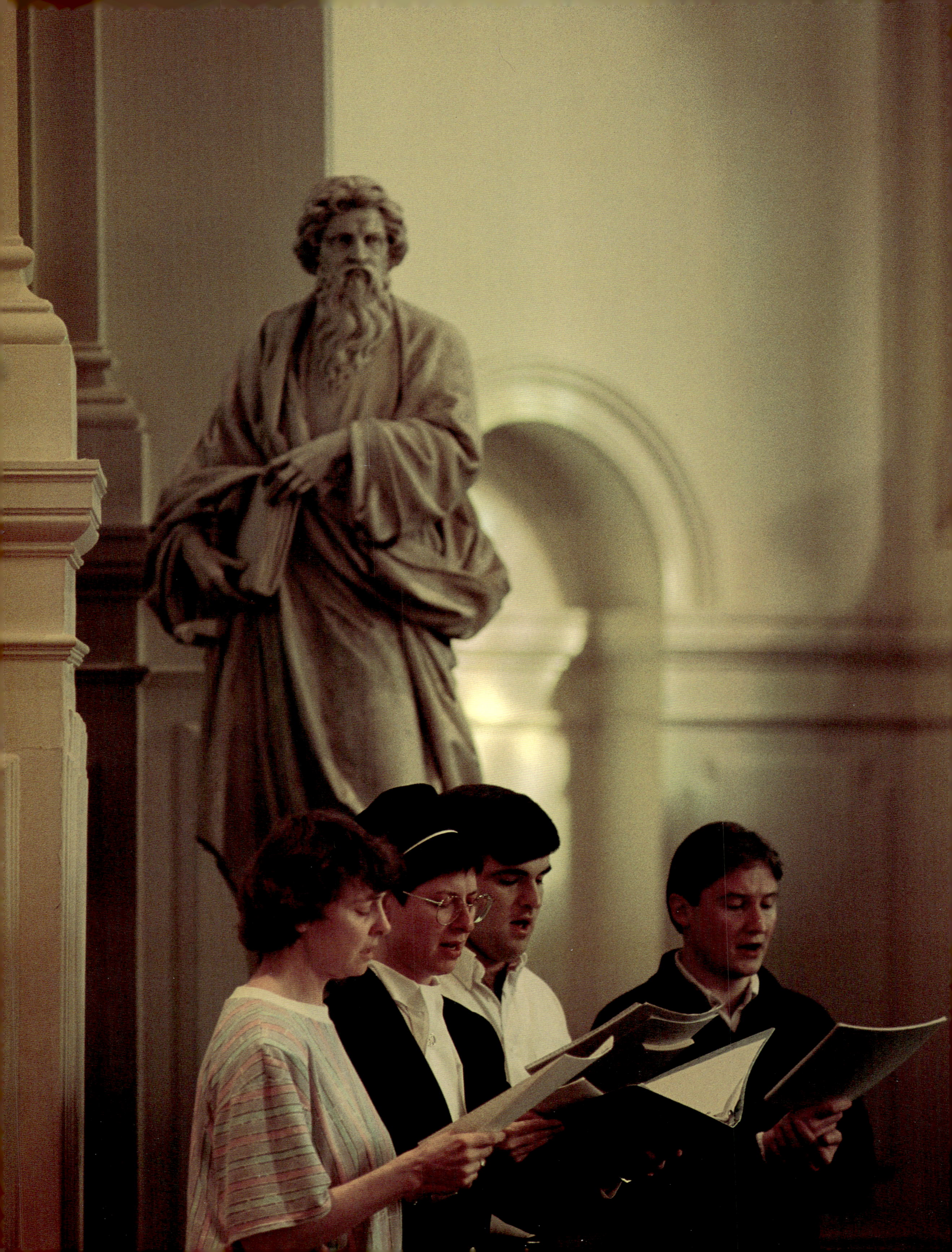

Left. A statue of Moses in Caldwell Hall's chapel watches over worshipers attending Mass.

Above. The Rev. William J. Byron, s.j., 12th president of The Catholic University of America, takes a few minutes from his busy schedule for contemplation.

Above. Jordon Rodgers of Washington, D.C., a graduate student in architecture, describes his urban design studio project to faculty critics Neal Payton, assistant professor of architecture, and Joseph Miller, professor emeritus of architecture, during a review session at the Edward M. Crough Center for Architectural Studies.

Right. Anticipating a faculty review, architecture students attach drawings of their studio design projects to the Crough Center's walls. The architecture curriculum offers many options, including dual-degree programs, summer sessions, and traveling studies programs.

Whatever might be its corporate imperfections and your private complaints, The Catholic University of America will have served you well by its continued commitment to include teaching about the morally good as well as the scientifically true and the artistically beautiful.

James H. Billington
Director, Woodrow Wilson
International Center for Scholars
CUA Commencement 1983

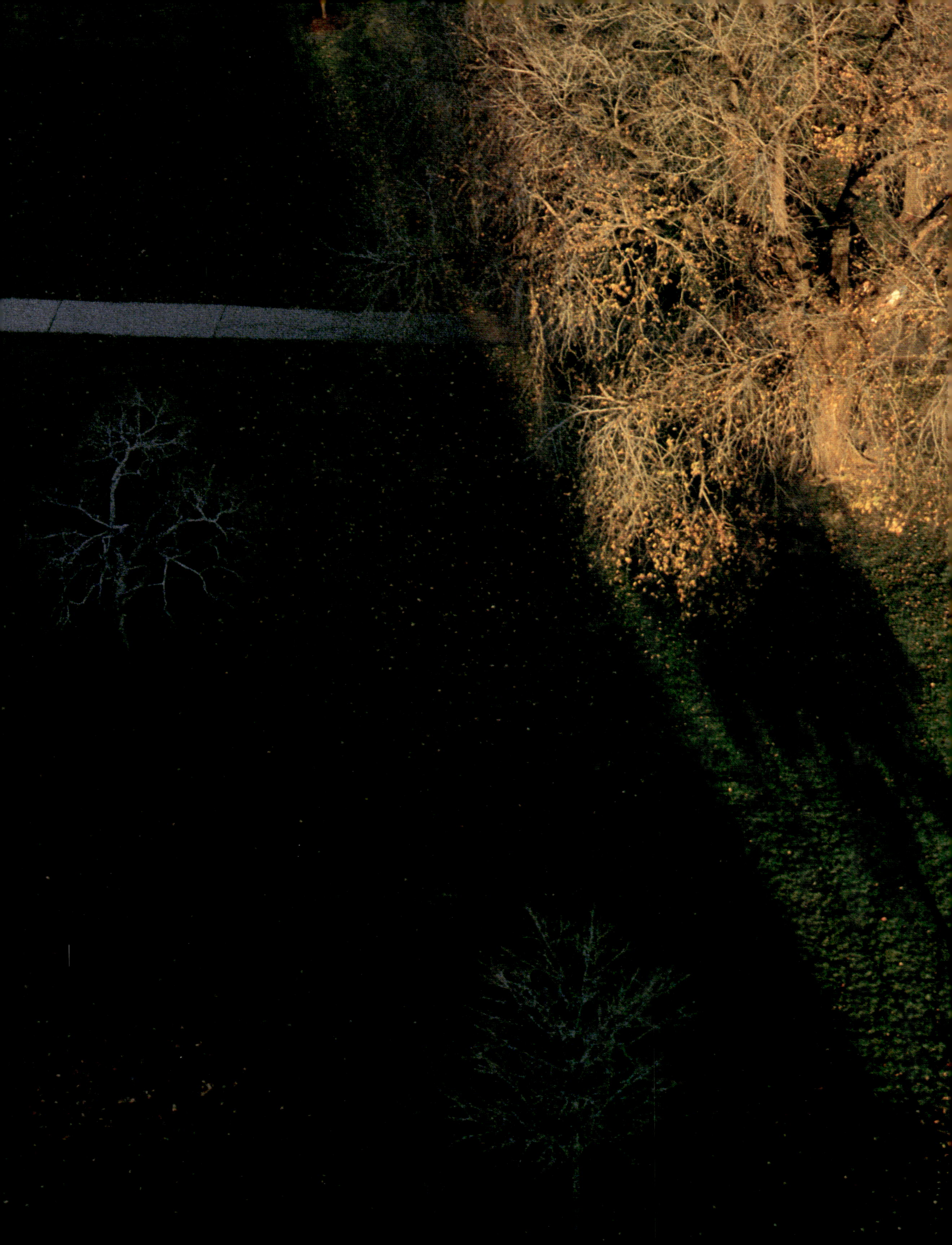

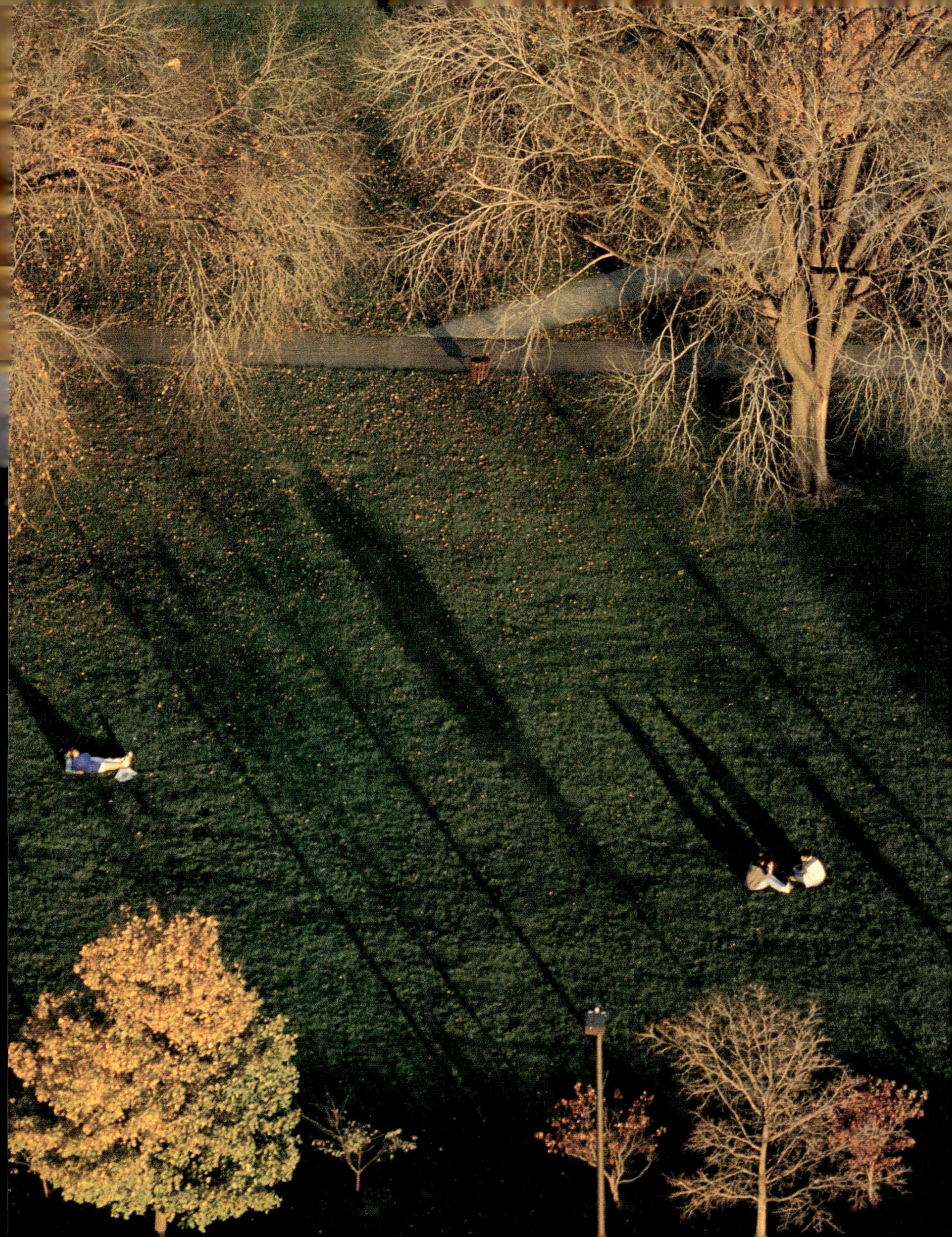

Pages 84-85. The spacious campus mall with its lofty trees and turf of greenery provides a perfect environment for conversation in the warm autumn sunlight.

Below. A class for majors at the music school emphasizes correct performance posture. The school is small enough to give students individual attention and large enough to provide opportunities for performing major musical literature for orchestra and chorus.

Right. Cellists Li Jie and Denise Setny ponder a passage during rehearsals at the Benjamin T. Rome School of Music. Li Jie of Shenyang, China, is a doctoral candidate in cello performance. Denise Setny, who has a master's degree in the same field, is active in the Washington music world.

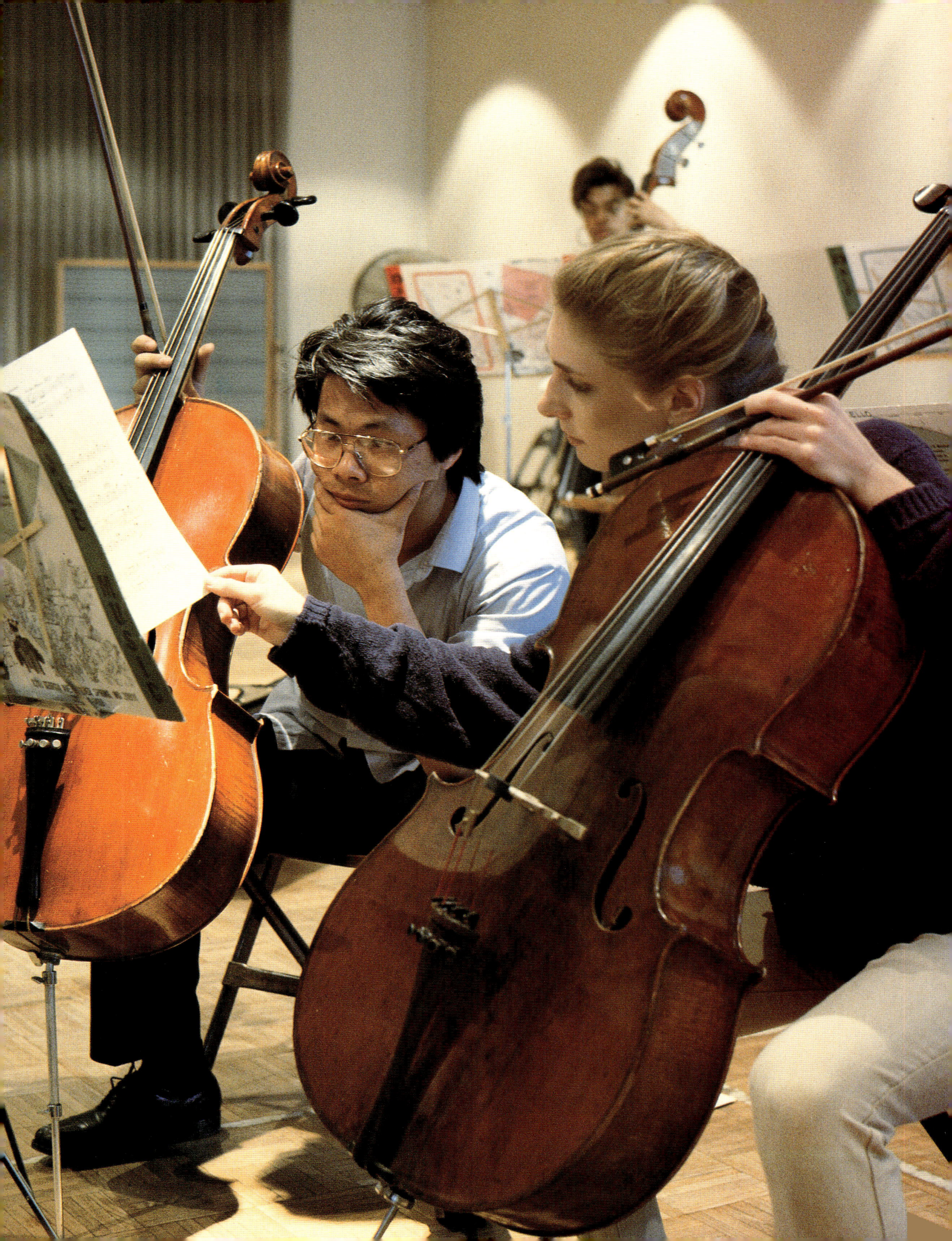

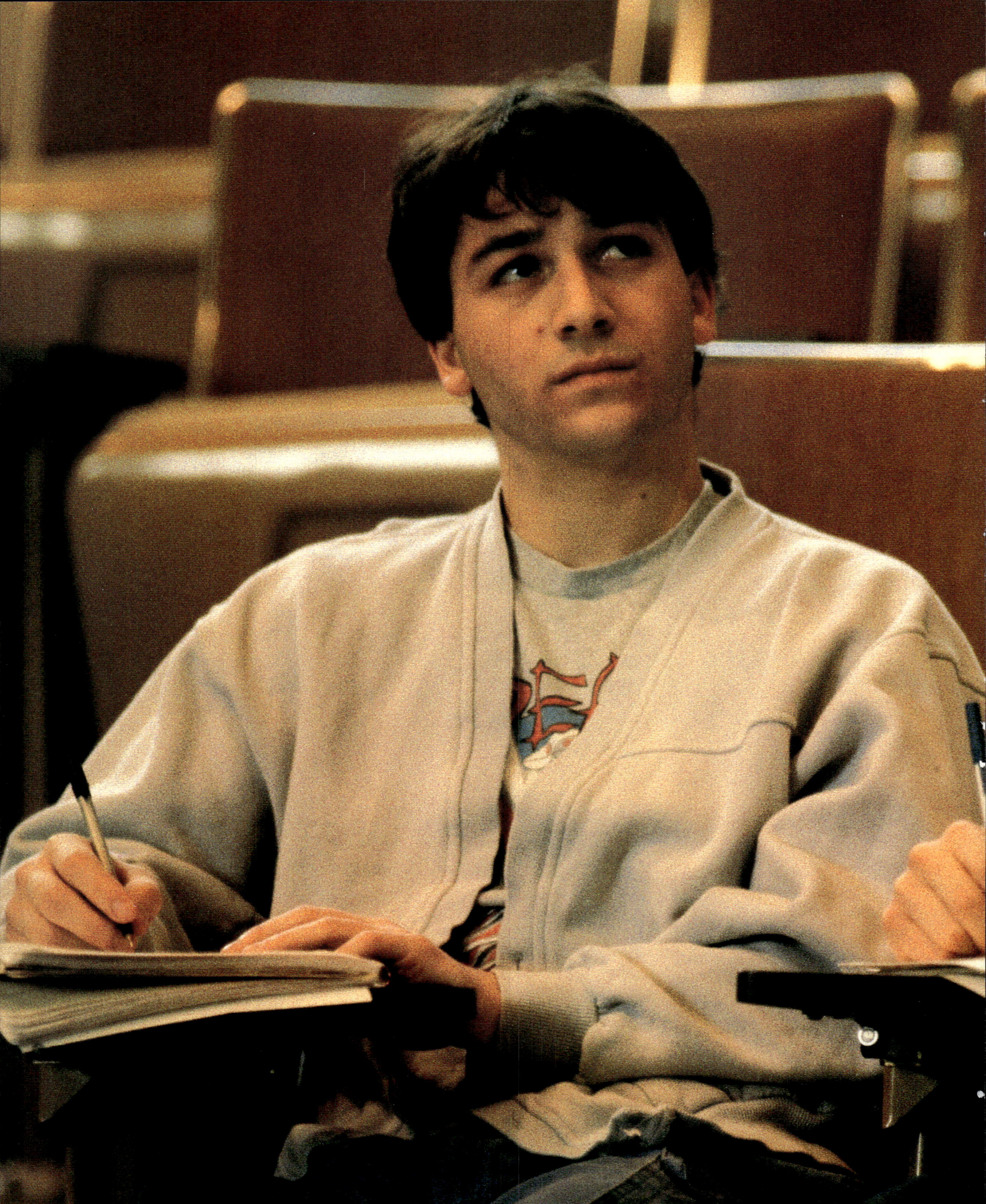

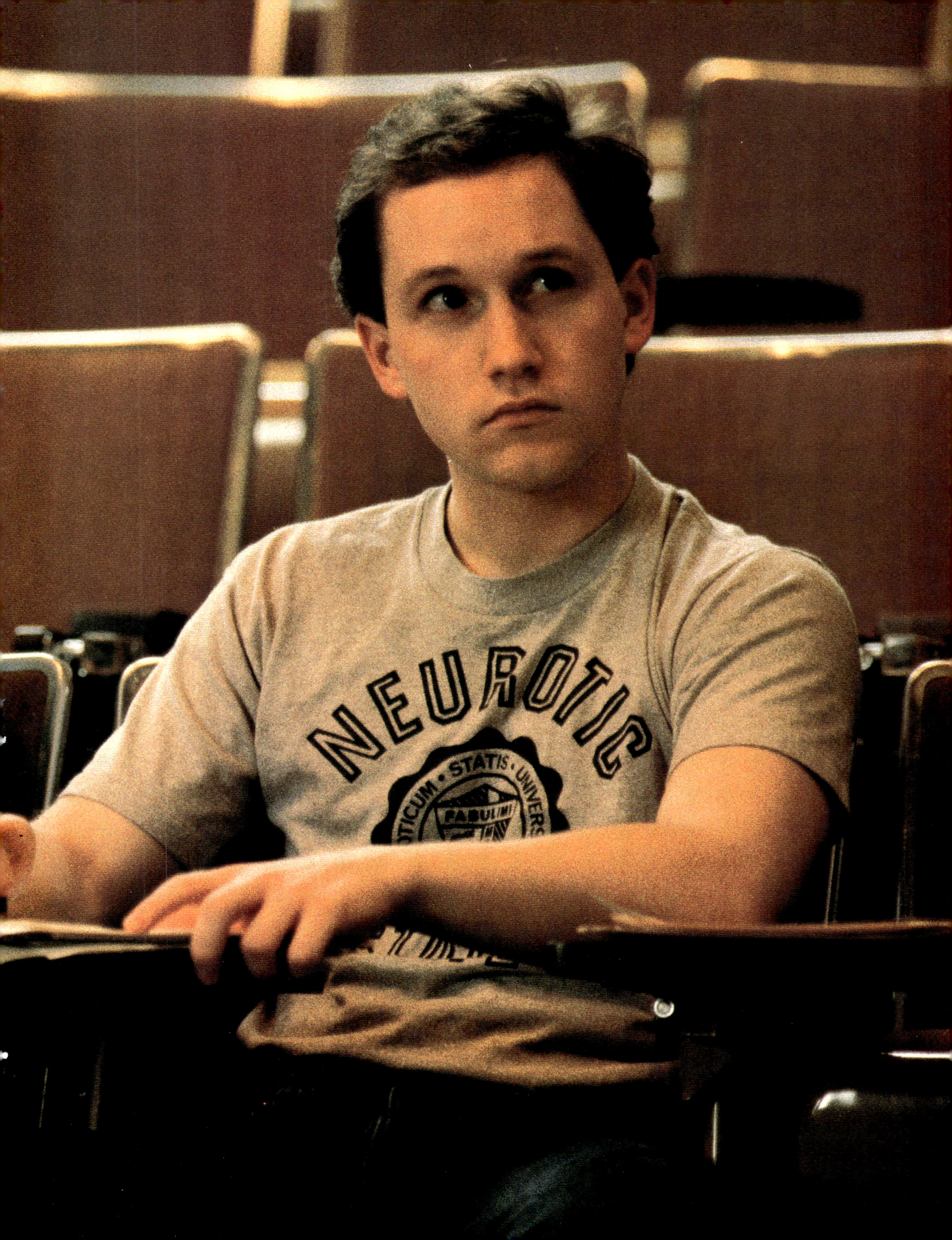
NEUROTIC
STATIS

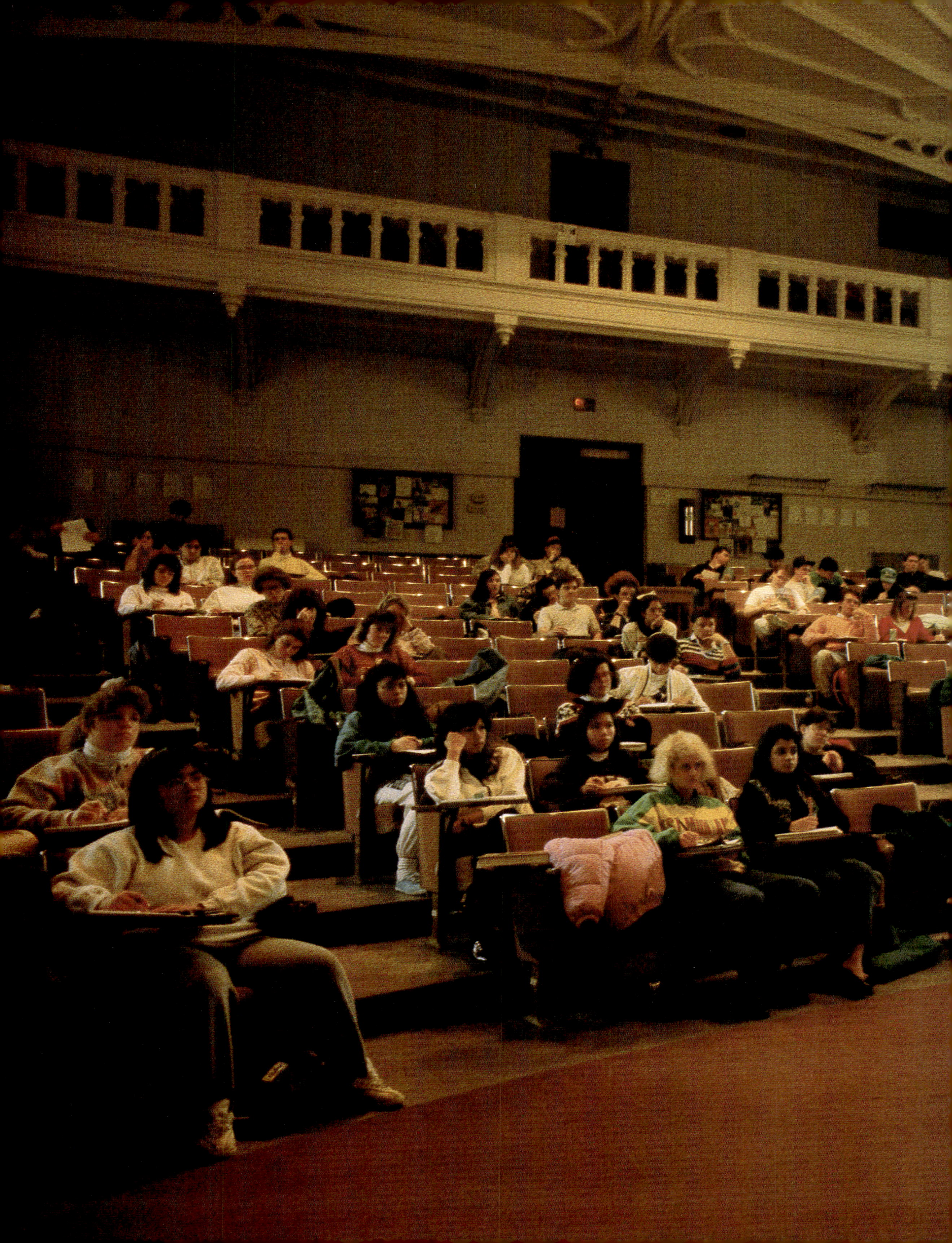

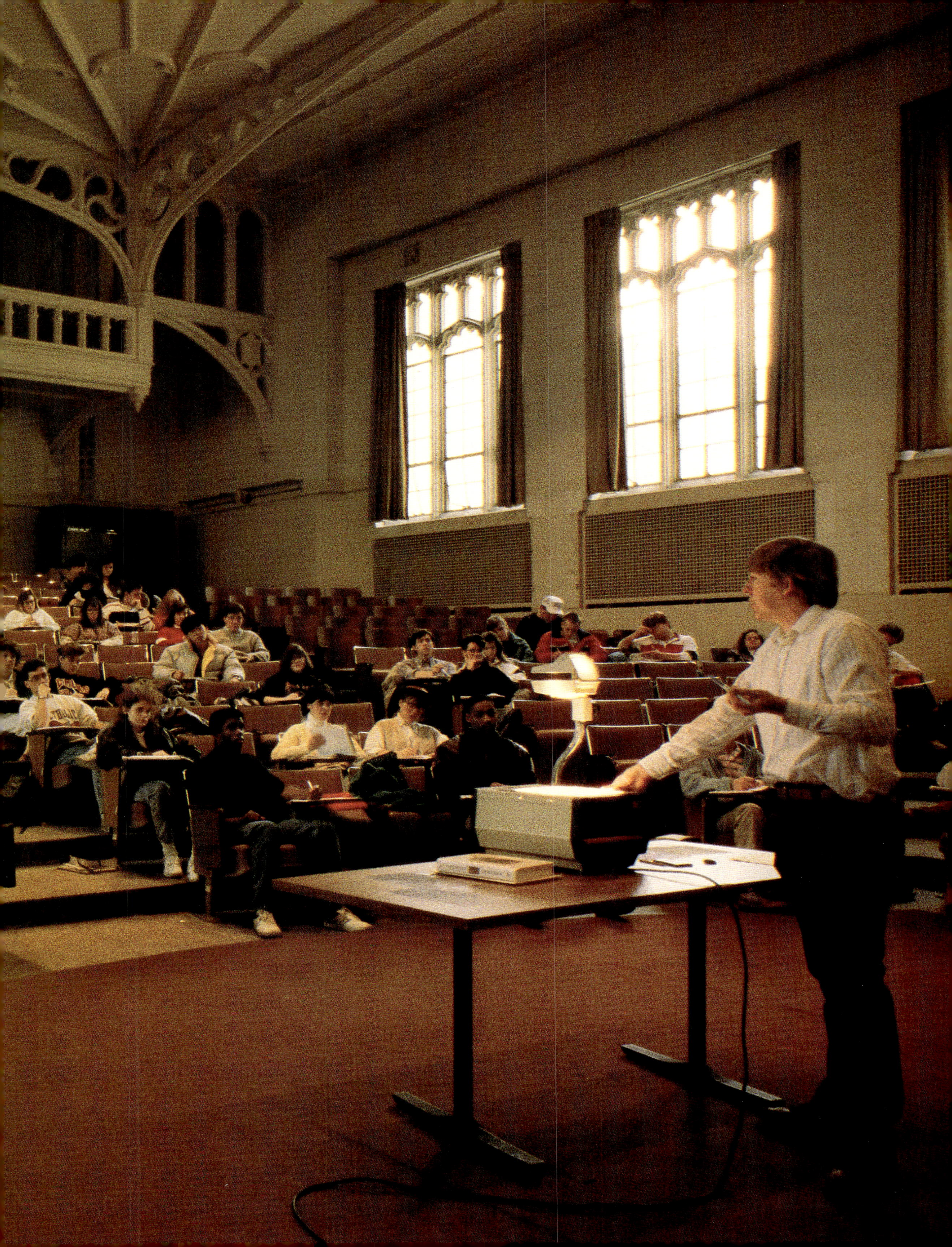

Pages 88-89. Psychology majors Scott DelBoccio of Holmdel, N.J., and Charles Judge of Bowie, Md., concentrate on a chemistry lecture in Maloney Hall, officially the Martin Maloney Chemical Laboratory, named for a Philadelphian.

Pages 90-91. Assistant Professor Gregory Brewer lectures to a chemistry class in the auditorium of Maloney Hall, built in 1914 and the last collegiate Gothic building constructed on the University campus.

Above. Basketball fans root for their Cardinals squad during a game at the Raymond A. DuFour Athletic Center. The University emphasizes balance between academics and athletics, but academics come first.

Right. Point guard Tracey Cahill, a politics major from Middletown, N.J., shows her court prowess in tournament action against Marymount University.

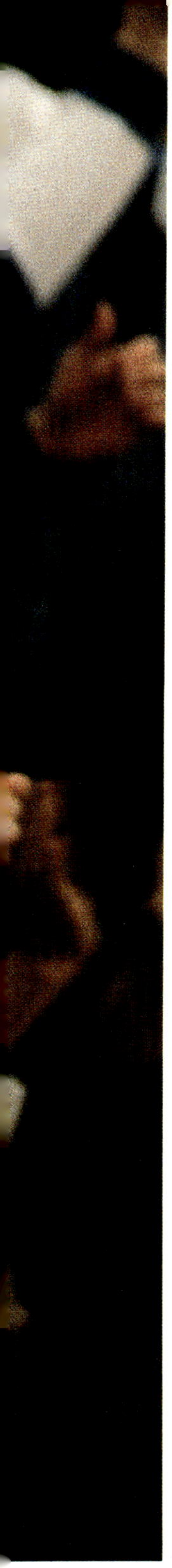

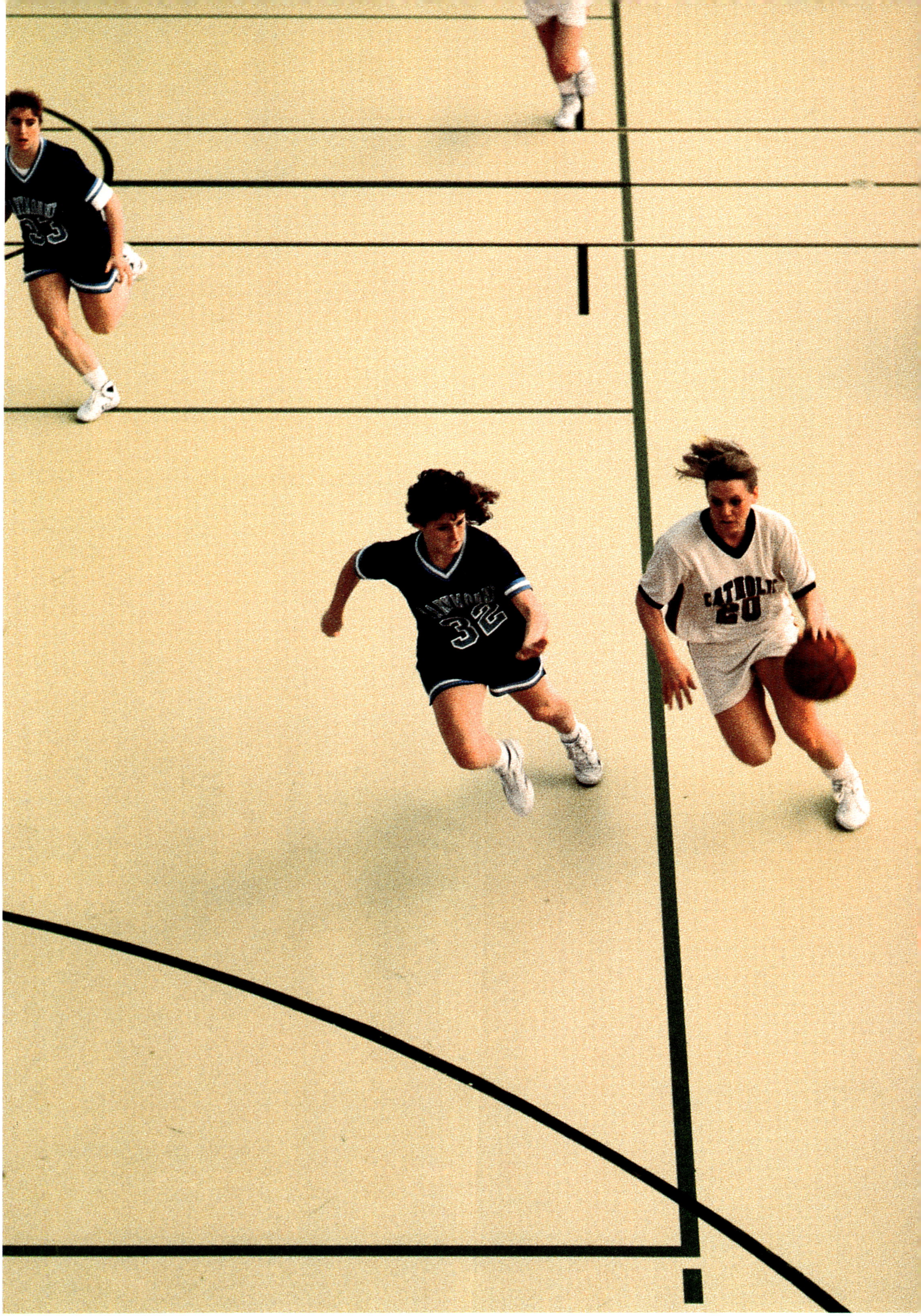
32
20

Below. Zach Lloyd, a psychology major from Prince Frederick, Md., takes a breather on the sidelines during a men's soccer contest.

Right. Cardinals running back Gary Lento of Kenosha, Wis., pumps iron to keep in shape, while defensive back Ben Clark of Dalton, Pa., serves as spotter. The Raymond A. DuFour Athletic Center's weight room offers fitness machines and free weights for the physical benefit of the University community.

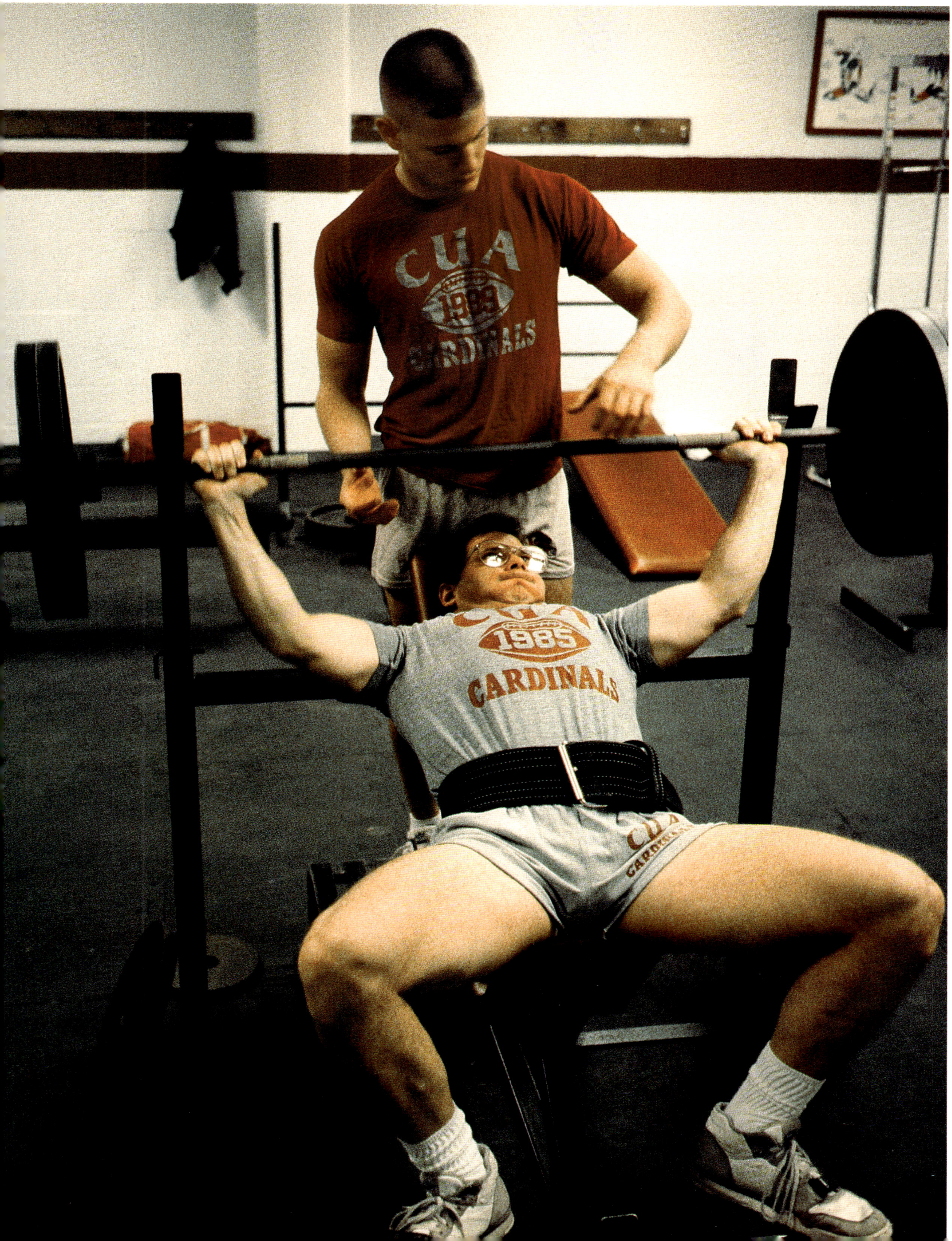
CUA
1989
CARDINALS
1985
CARDINALS
CUA

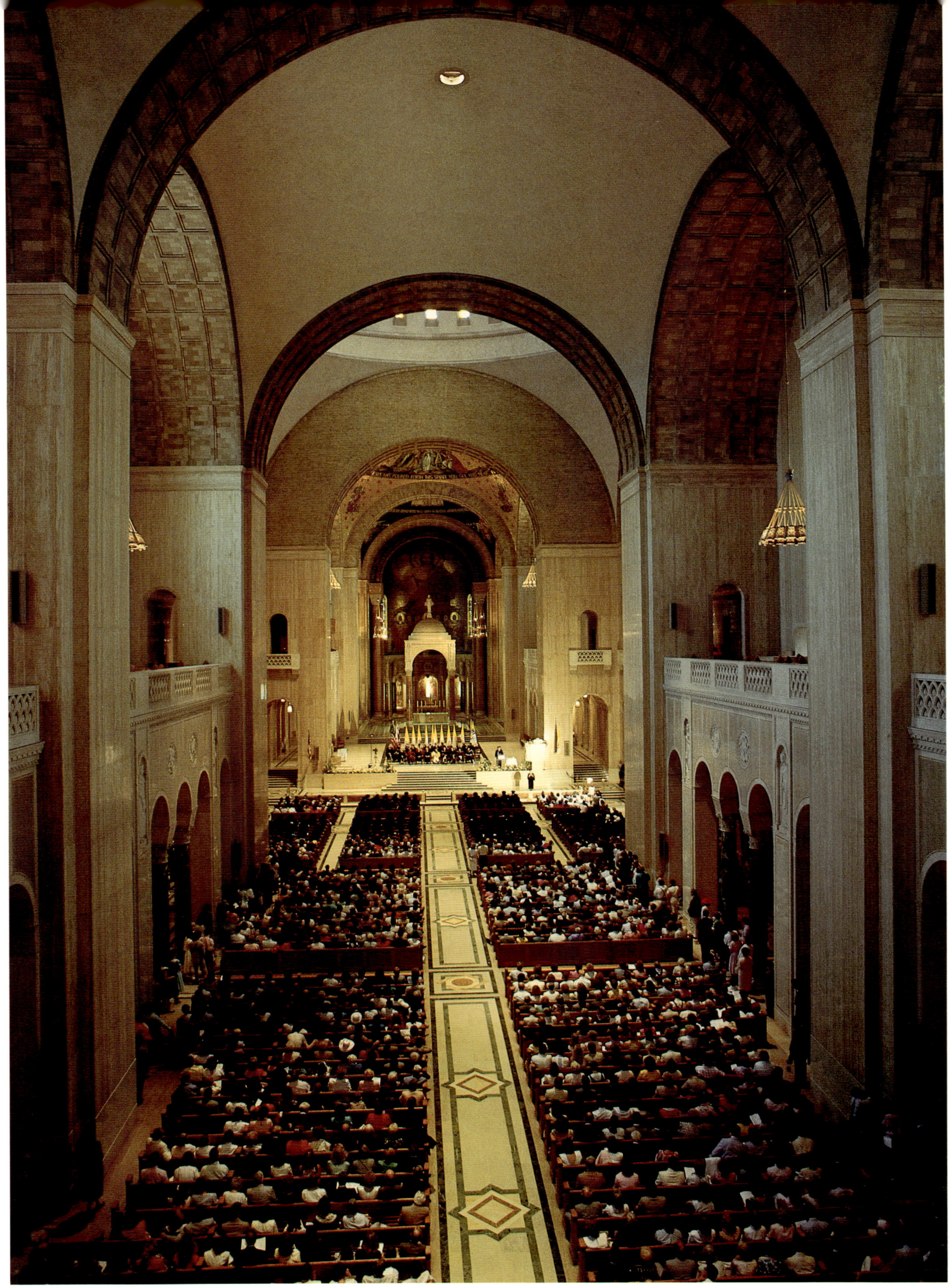

I cannot but feel at home with you.

Pope John Paul II
Oct. 7, 1979
visit to campus

Left. Law school graduates, their families and friends fill the Shrine's Upper Church on commencement day.

Above. Entertaining the Washington community at Christmastime are chorus members Joel A. Weiss, a music major from Clifton, Va.; Kelly Mancini, a musical theater major from Atlanta, Ga.; Ann T. Bergan, a psychology major from Havertown, Pa.; and Jennifer M. Sackmann, a musical theater major from Pleasantville, N.Y.

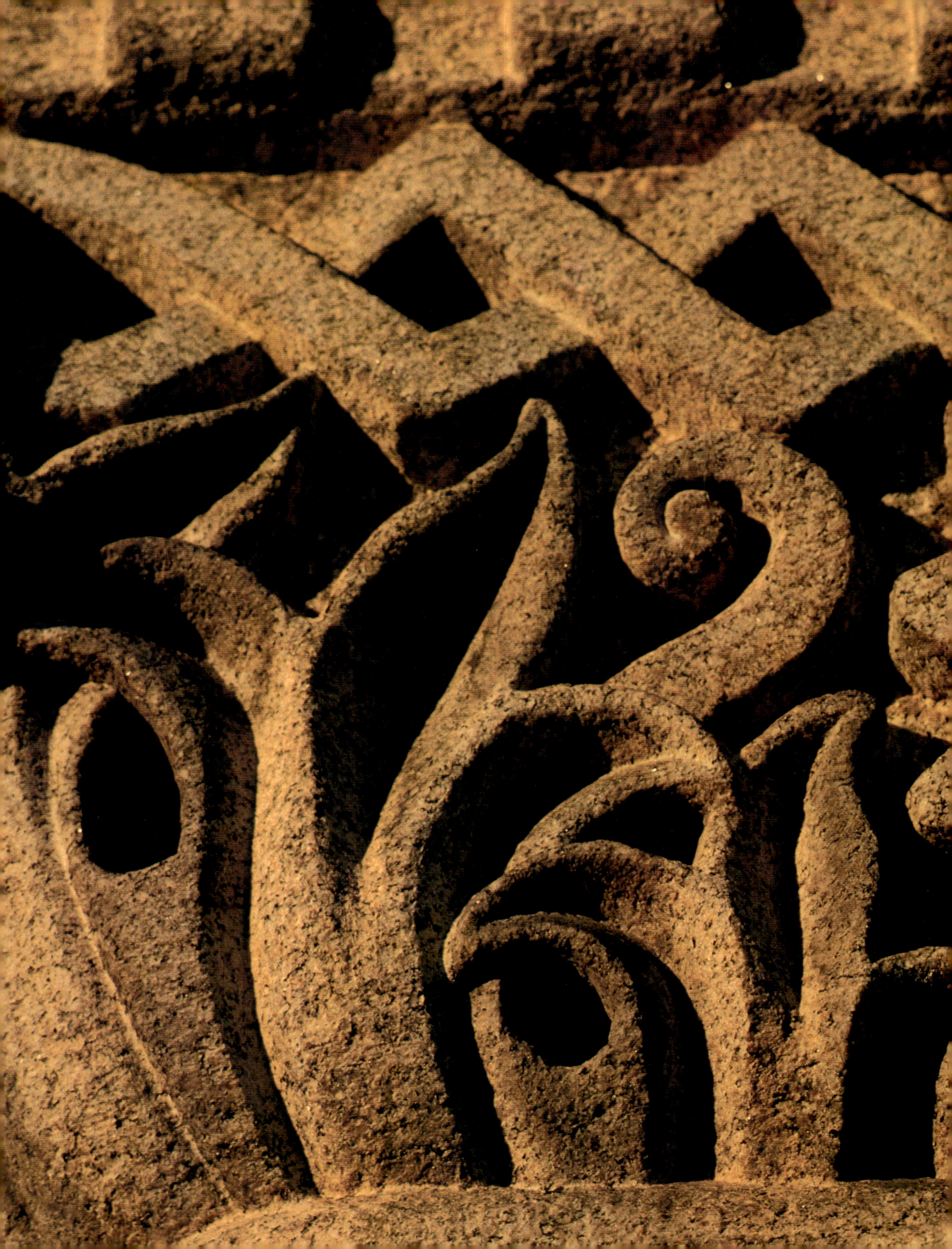

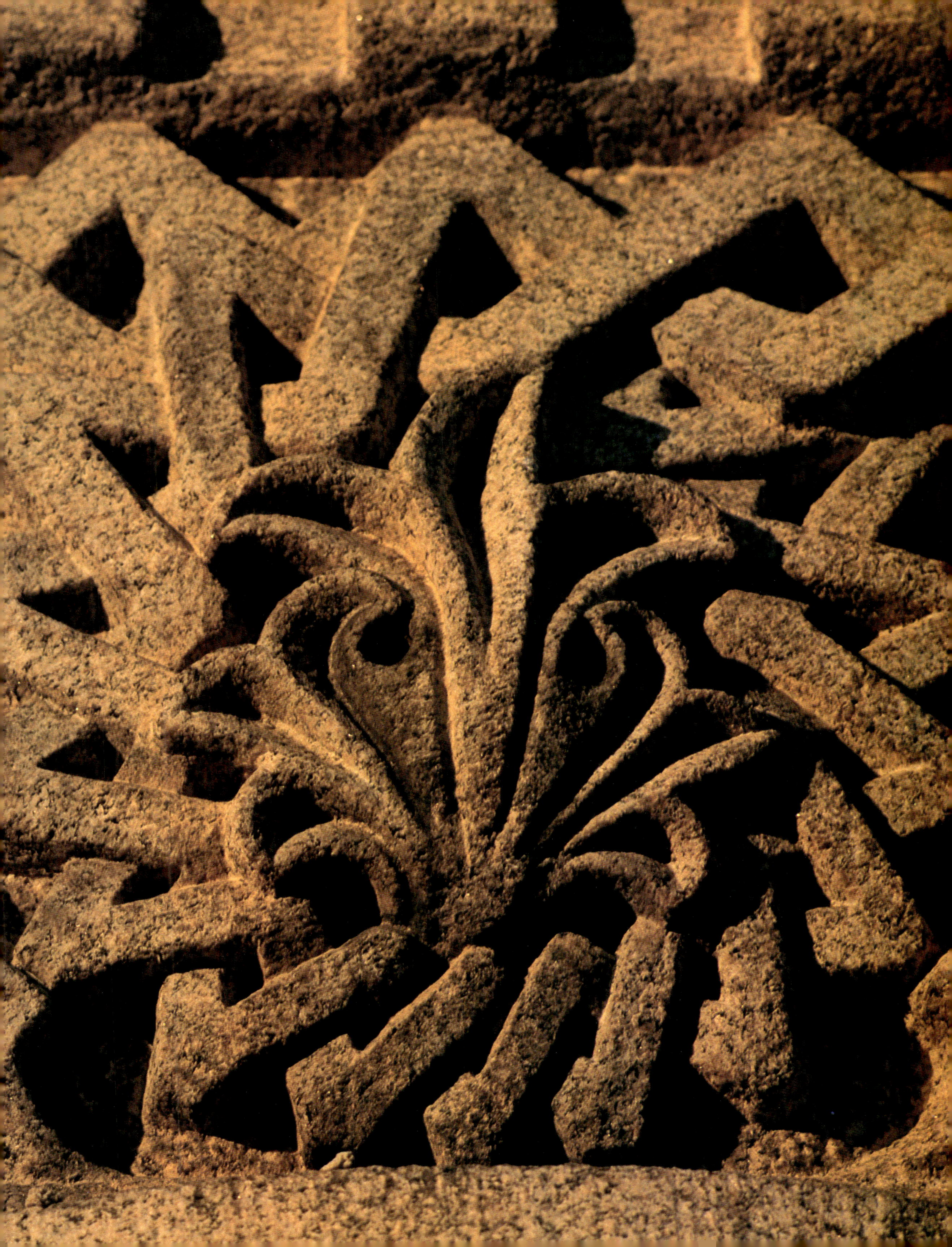

Pages 98-99. The weathered details of McMahon Hall symbolize the old, elegant and intricate process of learning.

Above. Small classes are a boon to students concentrating in science and technical fields. Listening closely to a science lecture are Robert T. Narh of Takoma Park, Md., a computer science major; and biology majors Marisa Wagner of Mechanicsburg, Pa.; Faith Devine of Red Bank, N.J.; and Christine Papa of Somerdale, N.J.

Right. Law Professor David A. Lipton discusses some of the finer points of securities regulations. Law school enrollment totals about 600 full-time and 250 part-time students.

$$\frac{\text{Capital}}{\# \text{Shrs}} = \text{par}$$

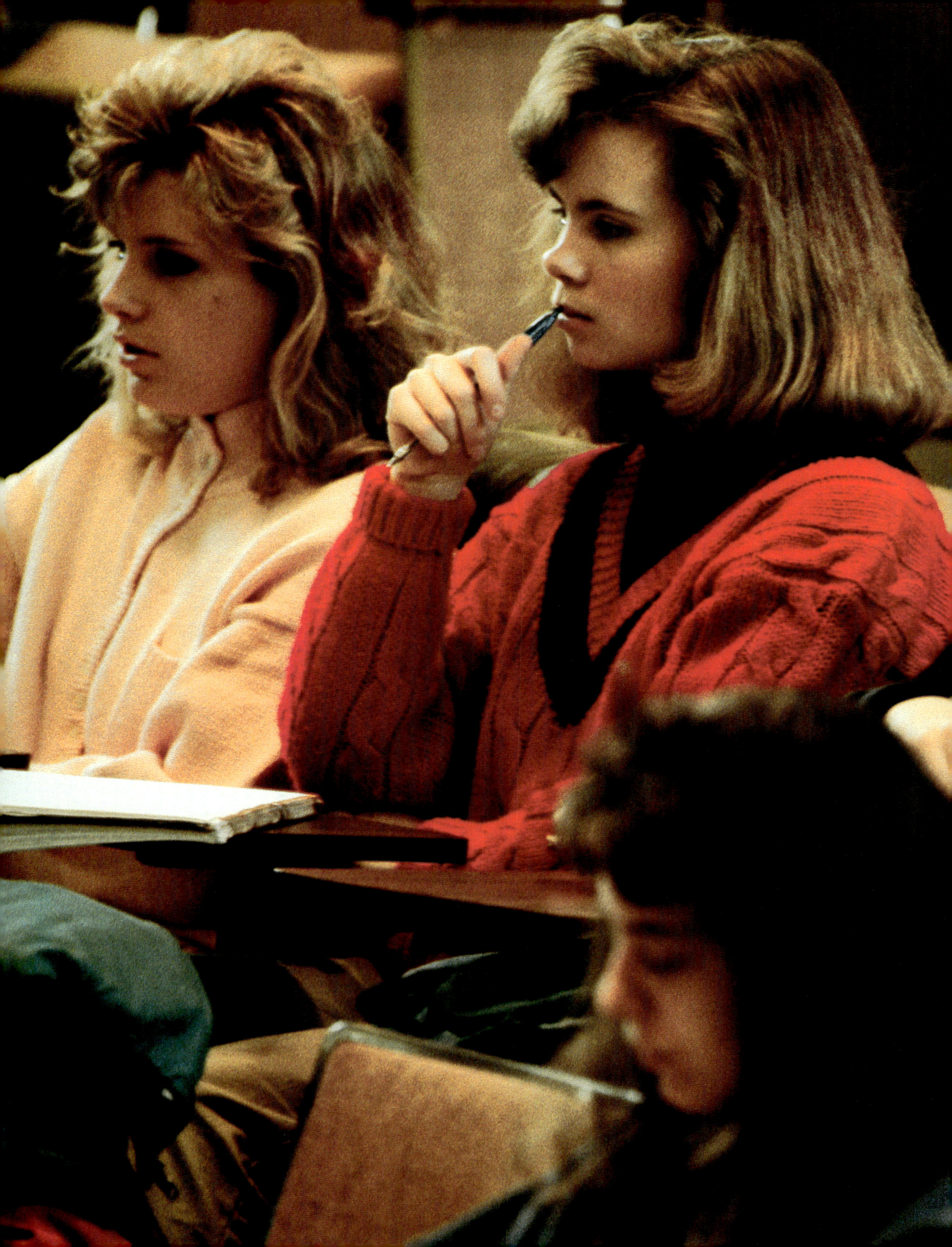

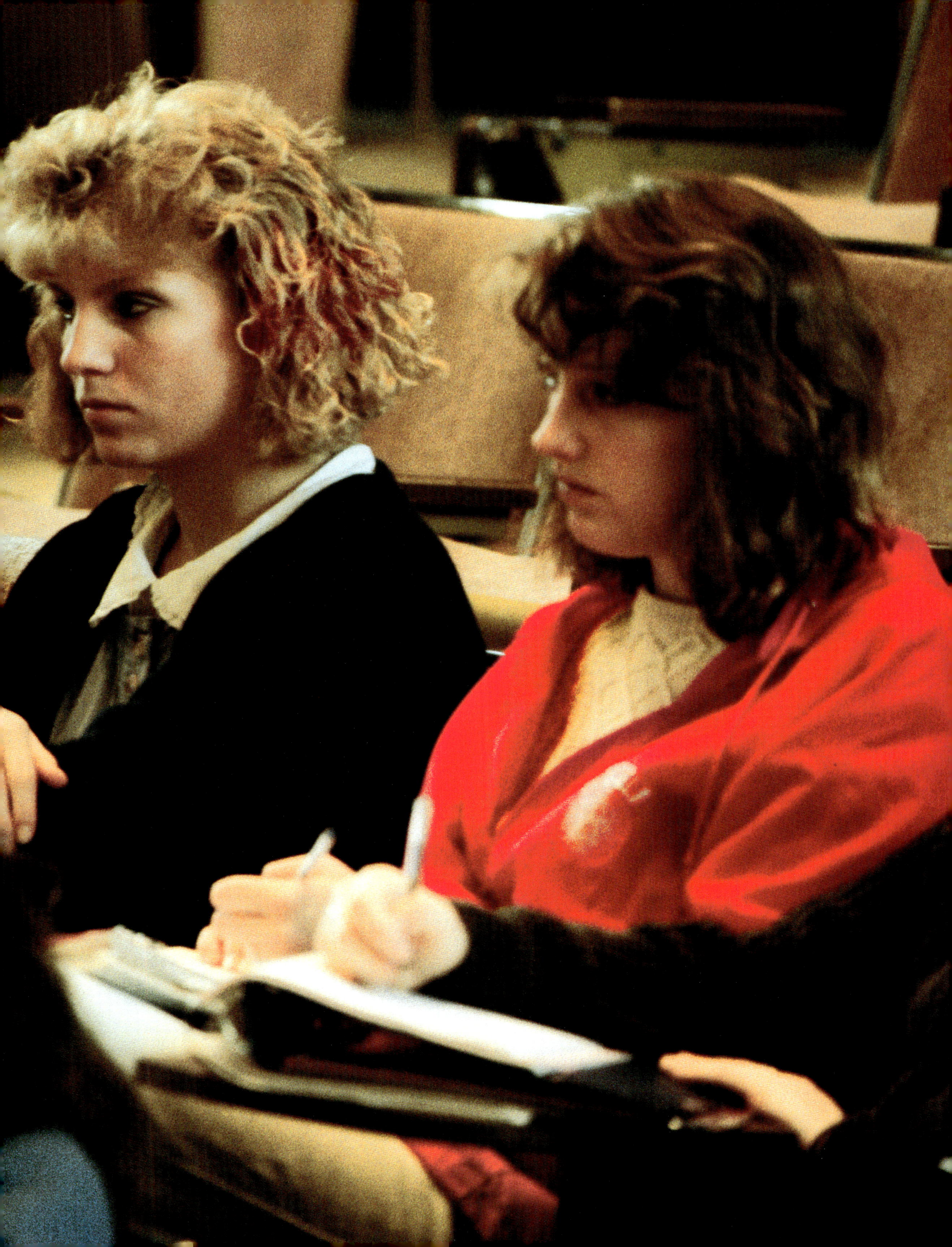

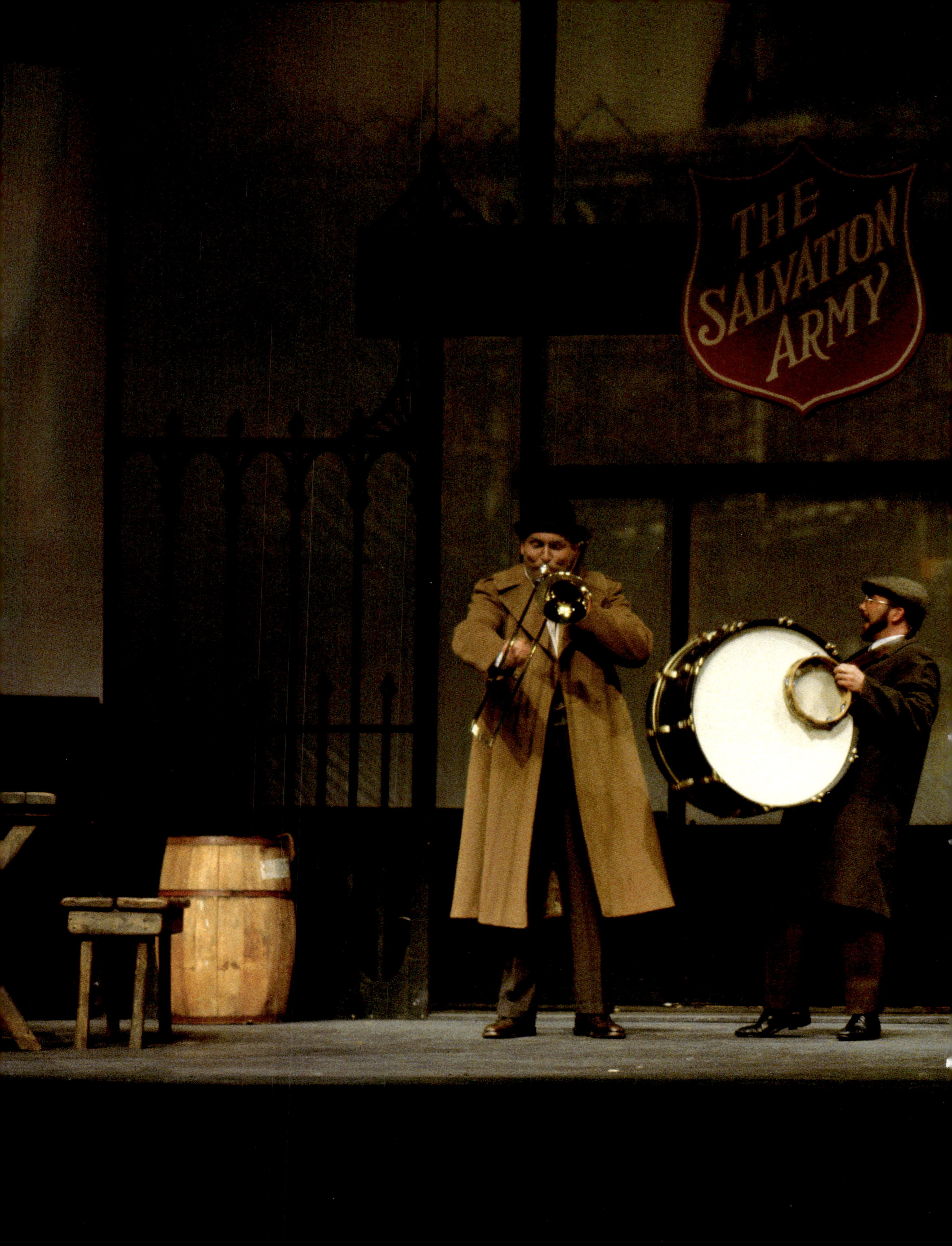
THE
SALVATION
ARMY

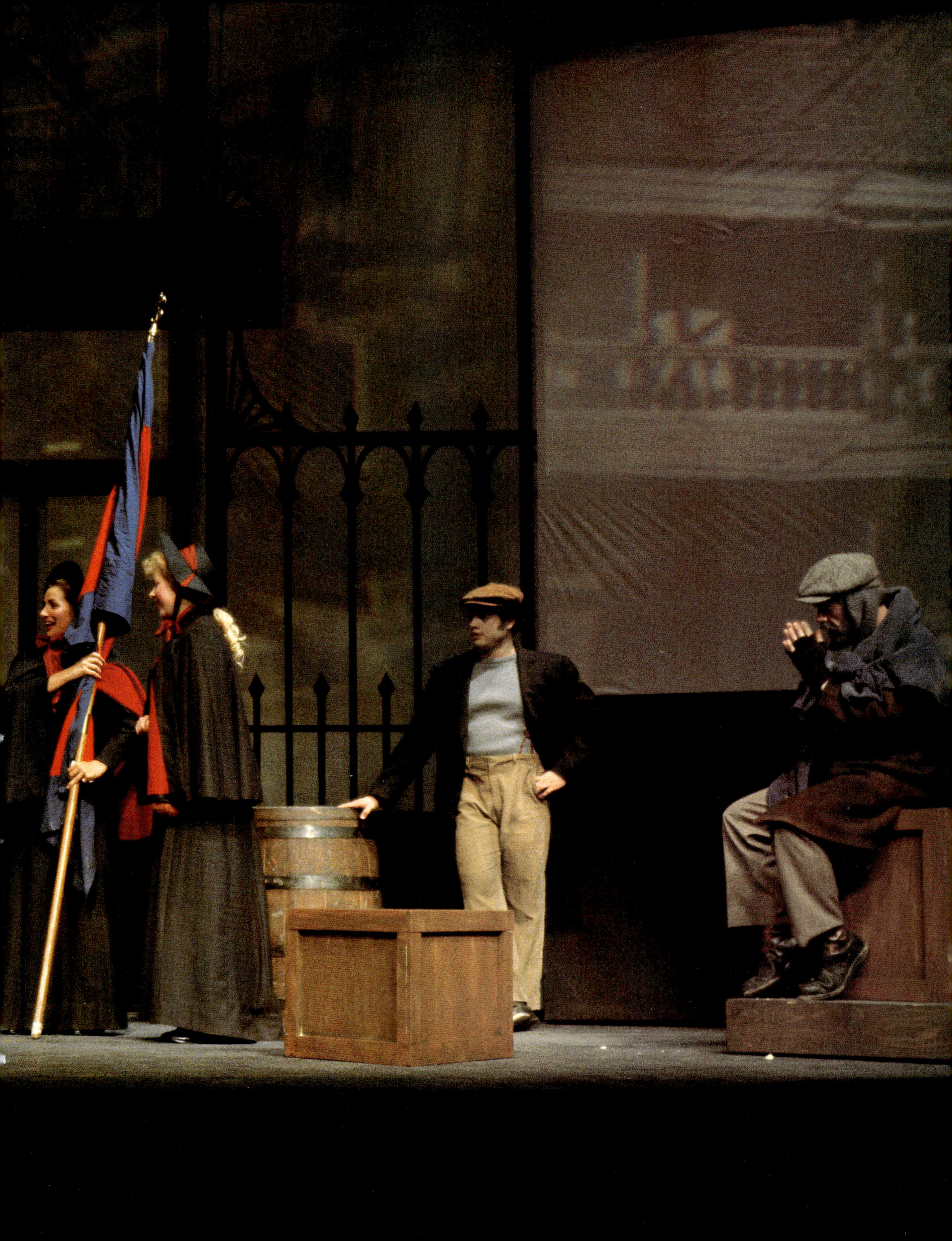

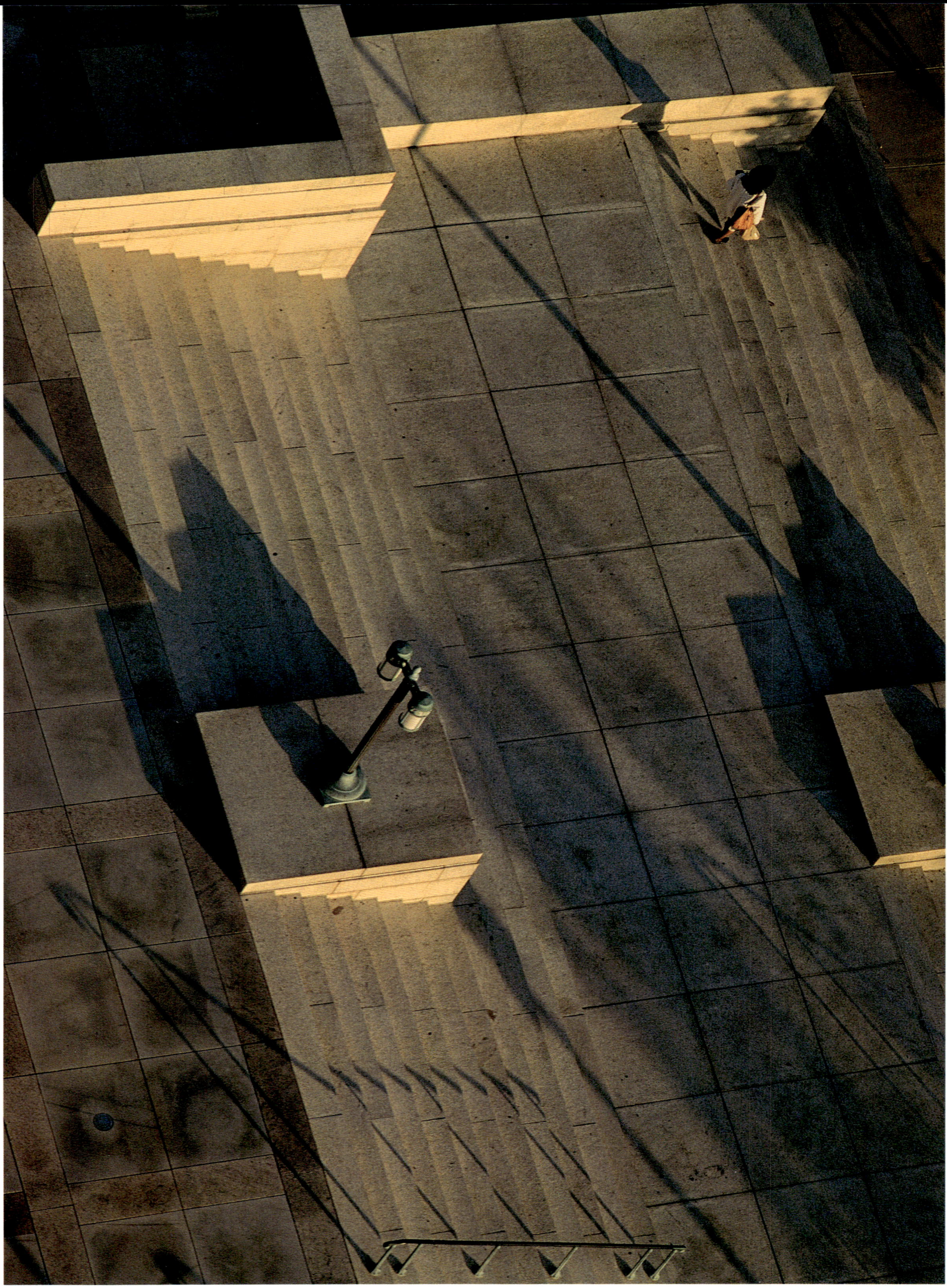

Pages 102-103. Listening to a lecture in Maloney Hall auditorium are nursing majors Amy Tracey of Medford, N.J.; Lynn Lilly of Fairport, N.Y.; Jody Trojan of Gallaudet University; Jennifer Staudenmeier of Furlong, Pa.; and (front) Therese Christofili of Tinton Falls, N.J. The School of Nursing is rated among the nation's "top 10" by deans of nursing schools.

Pages 104-105. Cast members of a Hartke Theatre production of George Bernard Shaw's *Major Barbara* assume the roles of Salvation Army band members.

Left. At day's end, long shadows slice across the main entrance to the Shrine.

Above. Faculty, students, alumni and well-wishers mix at reception following dedication of the Edward M. Crough Center for Architectural Studies.

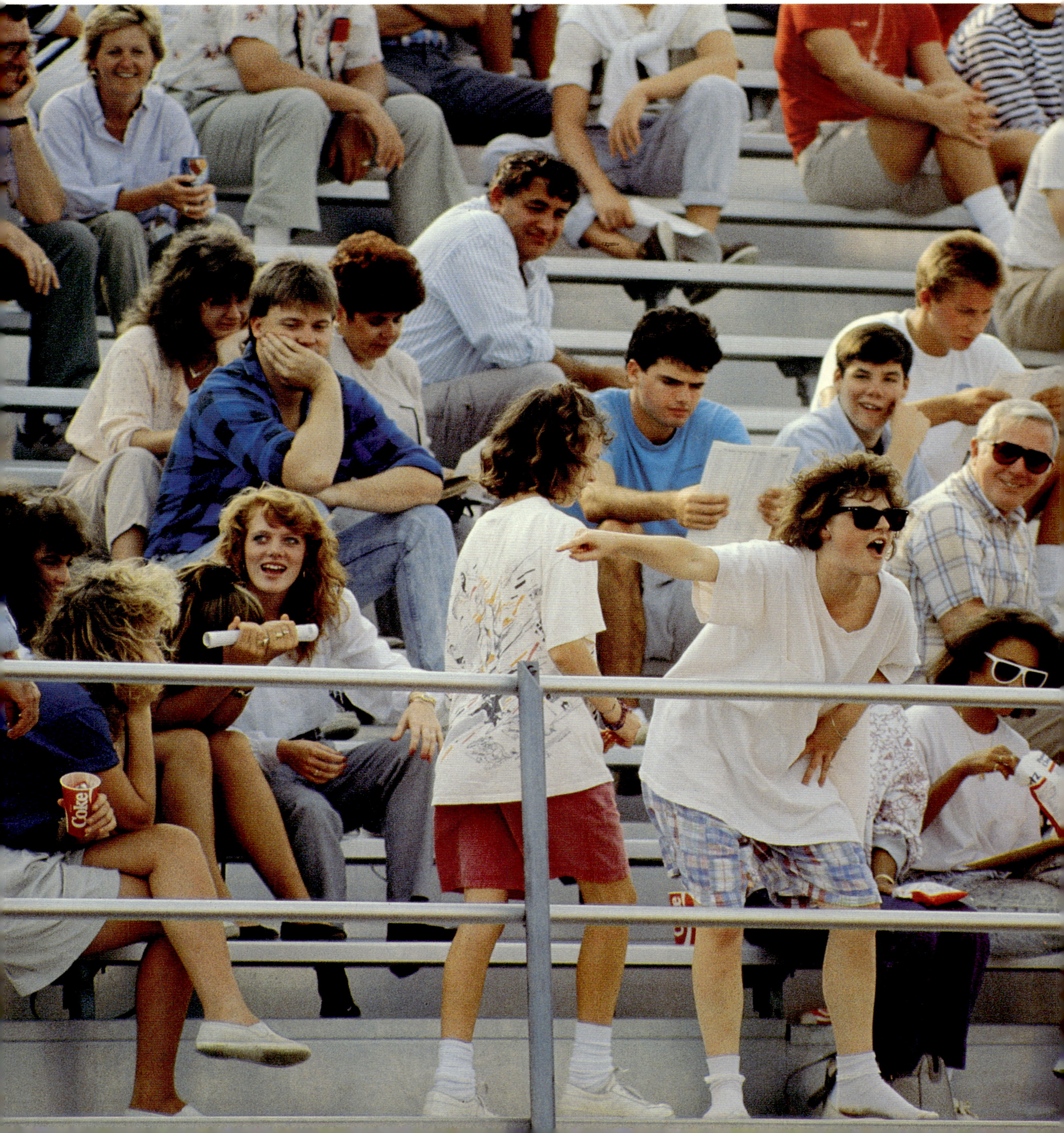
Coke

Left. The crowd enjoys watching the Cardinals football team. Participation in athletics is possible for a large number of students because the University is a member of NCAA Division III.

Above. Cardinals wide receiver David DeGeronimo of Milltown, N.J., catches a pass as Fordham defenders tackle.

If we bishops did not have such a University as The Catholic University of America, we would have to create one. Our forebearers did that for us. Our responsibility is to maintain and guide it.

Cardinal John Krol
1987 Centennial

Above. Biologist David Krause examines an experiment in the University's Vitreous State Laboratory, prominent in producing optical fiber and high-strength glass and material for safe nuclear waste disposal.

Right. An experiment begins in the laboratories of the biology department, which boasts an outstanding research faculty and is known for success in placing graduates in the nation's leading medical schools.

POWER
STIRRER POSITION
RESET
FILL
FOCUS
MANOMETER SELECT
STIRRER CONTROL

To develop a department or school in the creative arts, you must have a creative faculty and then mount professional productions. The proof is what you see on the boards.

The Rev. Gilbert V. Hartke, O.P.
Founding Chairman
Department of Drama

Left. Hair stylists perfect the coiffure for drama graduate student Alice O'Neill of Washington, D.C., as she prepares to make her appearance on stage at Hartke Theatre. She performed in the theatre's productions of Tennessee Williams' *The Glass Menagerie* and Howard Brenton's *Bloody Poetry*.

Right. "Broadway Night" performer Cheryl Powell Muniz dances across the stage at Hartke Theatre, which actress Helen Hayes chose for her last stage performance in *Long Day's Journey Into Night*.

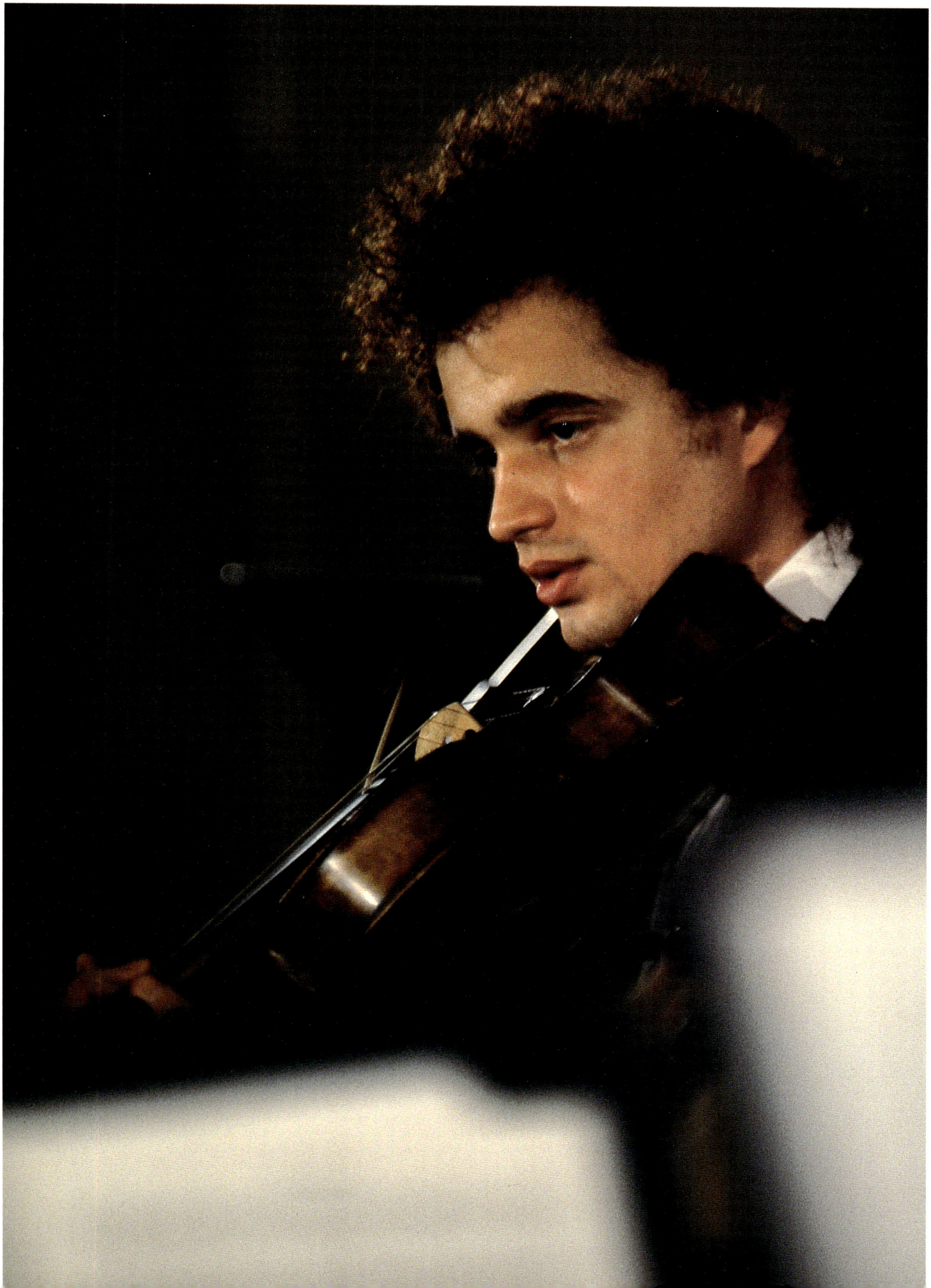

I am often asked if my architecture training has influenced my photography, and of course it has. Architecture studies, in addition to providing a professional degree, offered a great liberal arts education.

Fred J. Maroon
Century Ended, Century Begun
1990

Left. From detailed drawings to scale models, ideas by architects take shape. For his cultural intervention studio project, Tom Krizmanic of Monona, Wis., designs a proposal for a historic district in Nimes, France.

Below. Architecture students got a home of their own when the "Old Gym" became the sparkling Edward M. Crough Center for Architectural Studies, named for the 1950 civil engineering alumnus.

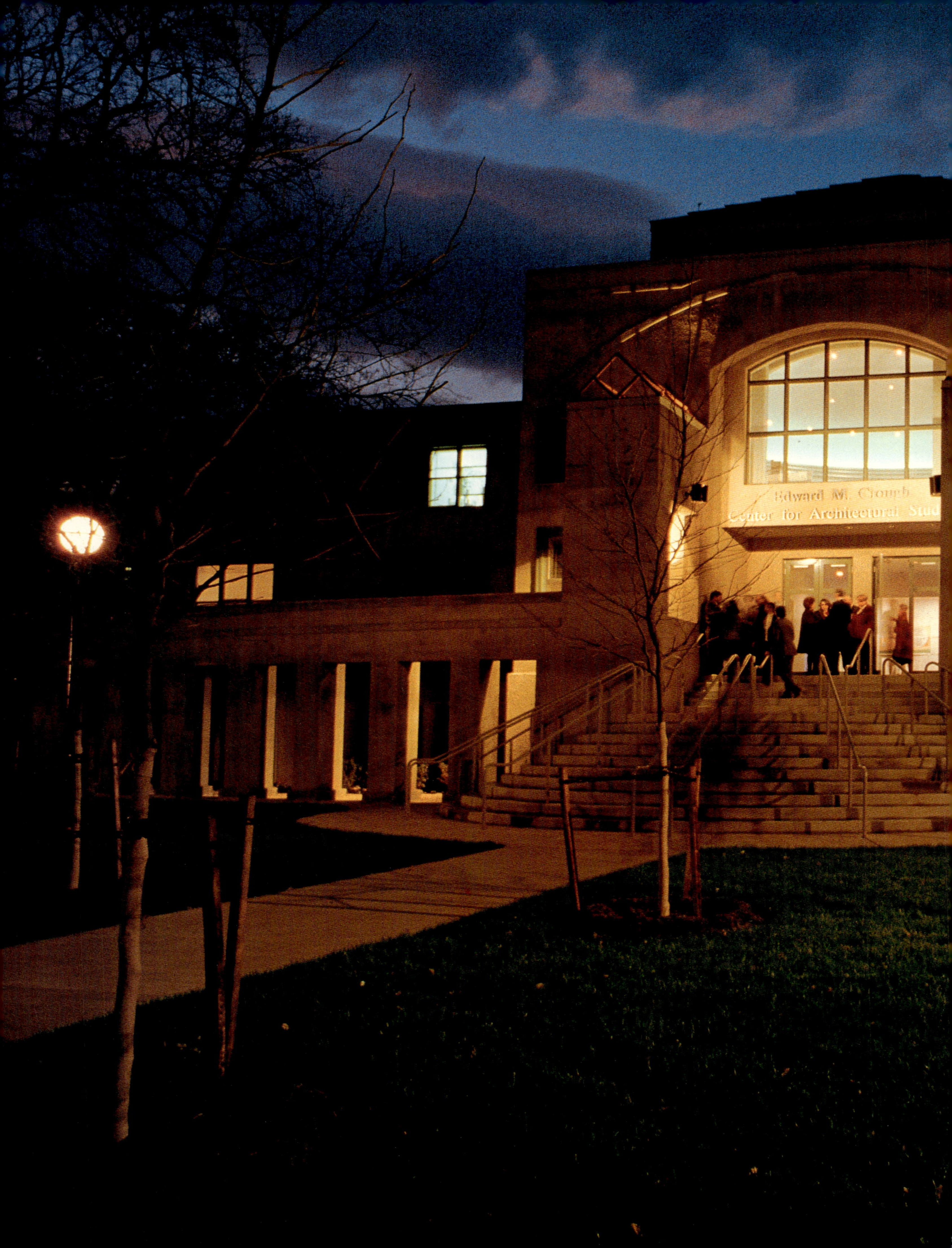
Edward M. Crough
Center for Architectural Stud

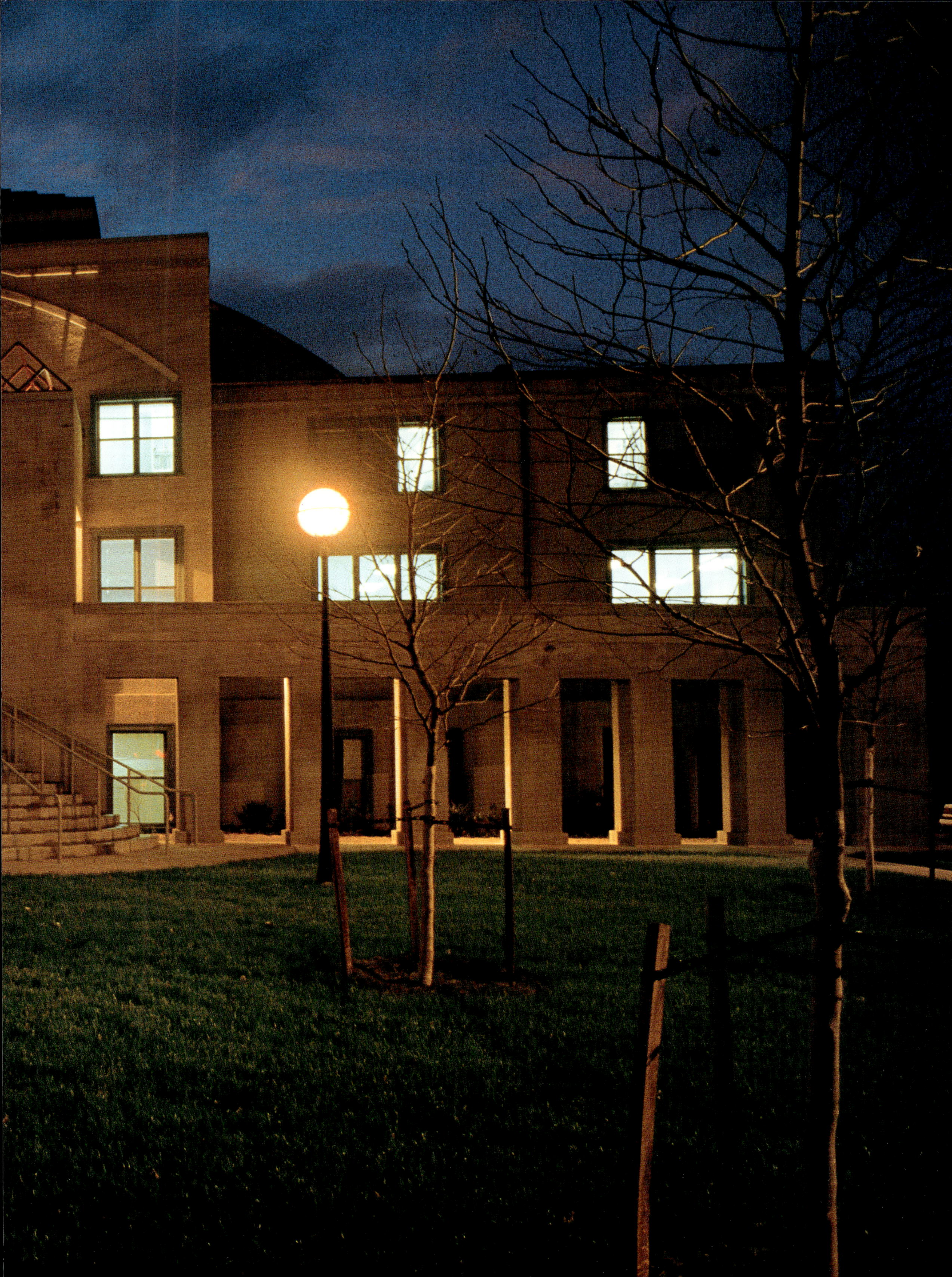

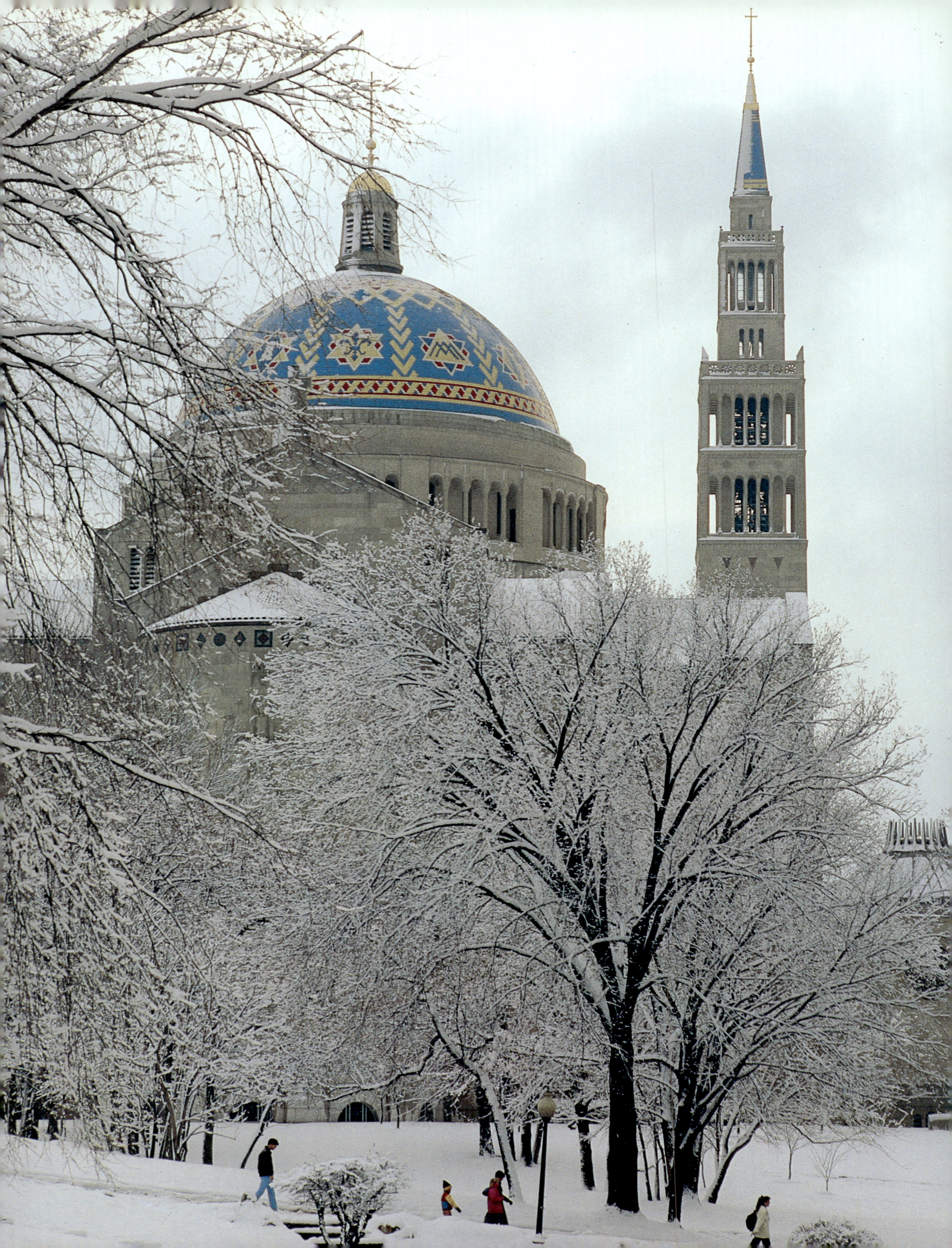

Pages 52-53. Twilight gives the Edward M. Crough Center for Architectural Studies a chance to show another side of its resplendent luster.

Left. The gold, blue and red dome of the Shrine and the Knights' Tower, with 56 carillon bells, rise from the snowy blanket covering the campus. Former University Trustee John McShain built the Upper Church and regarded it as the "greatest project" he ever undertook. Cardinal Patrick O'Boyle, former archbishop of Washington and University chancellor, guided the Upper Church's construction.

Above. The rose window above the Shrine's main entrance features gold and amethyst accents associated with Byzantine architecture. Unlike rose windows in Gothic architecture, the Shrine's windows are in a wheel pattern with heavy stone spokes radiating from the center.

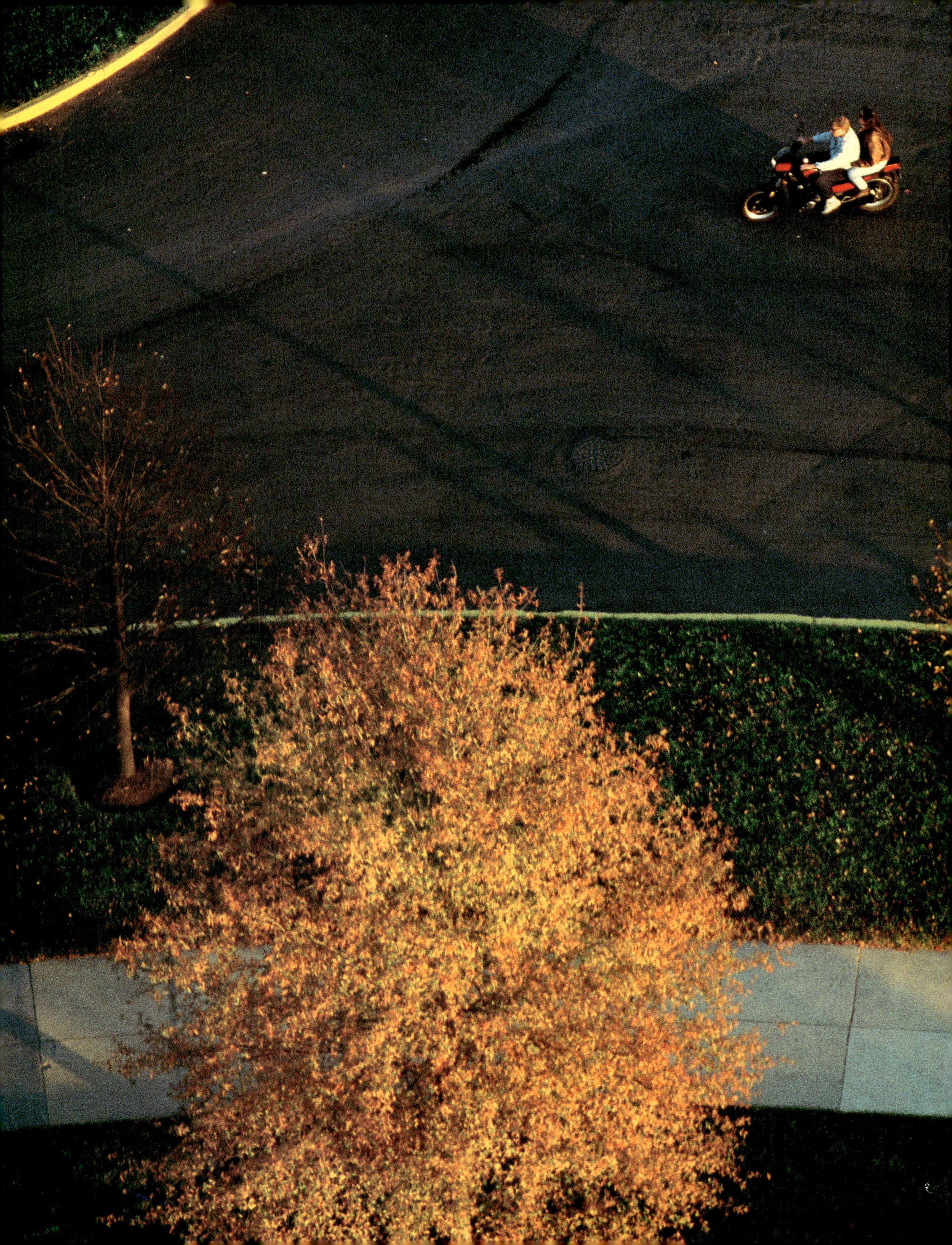

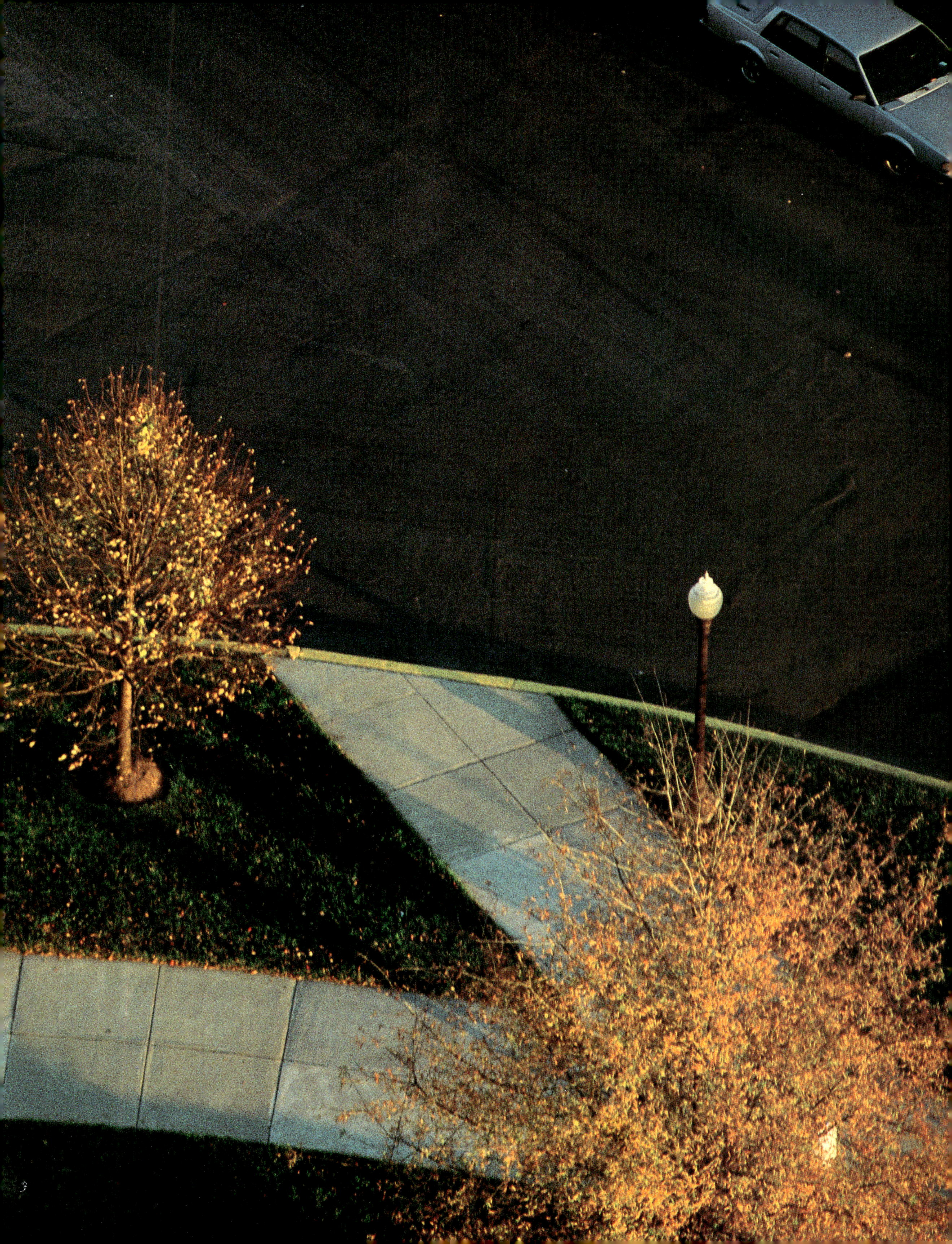

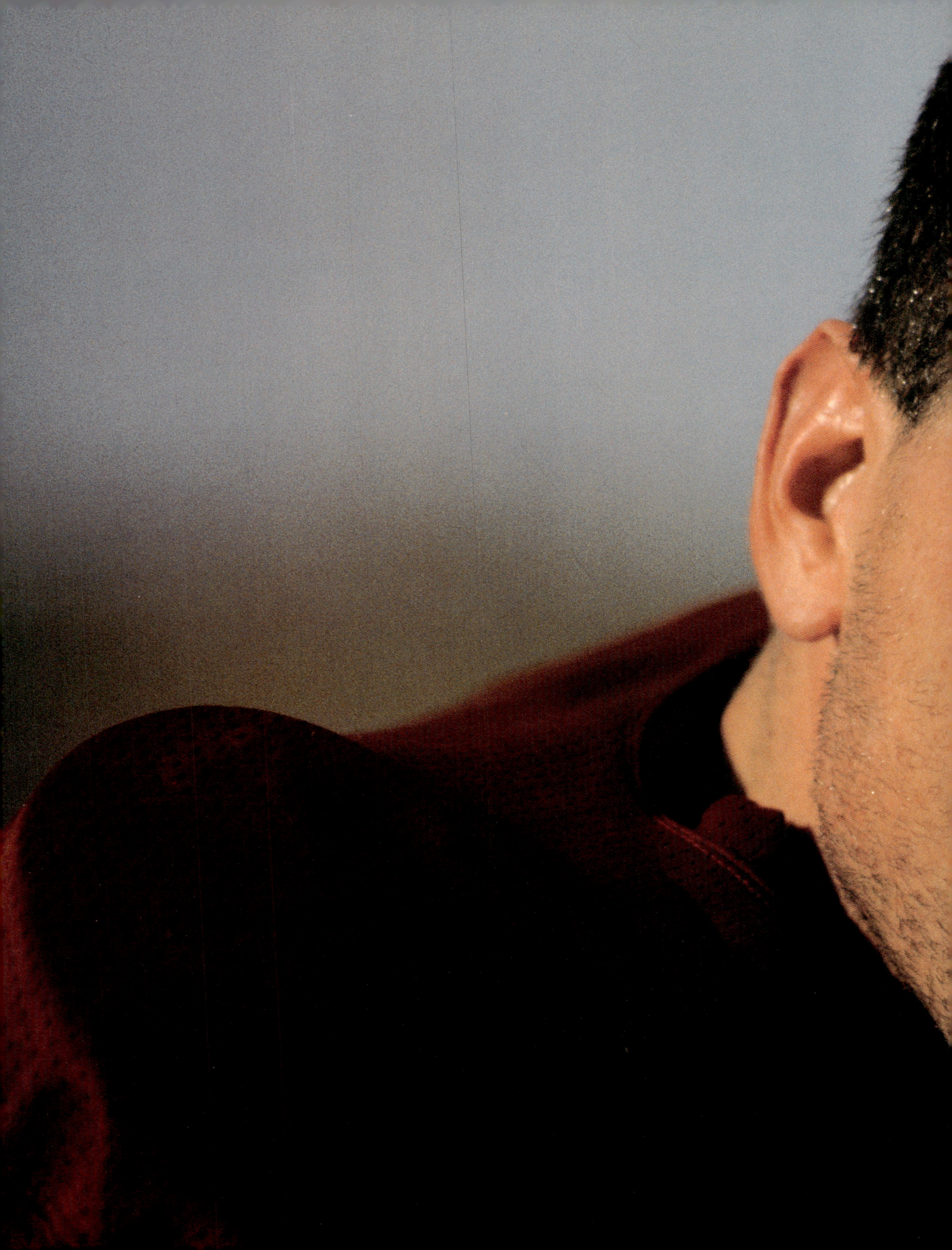

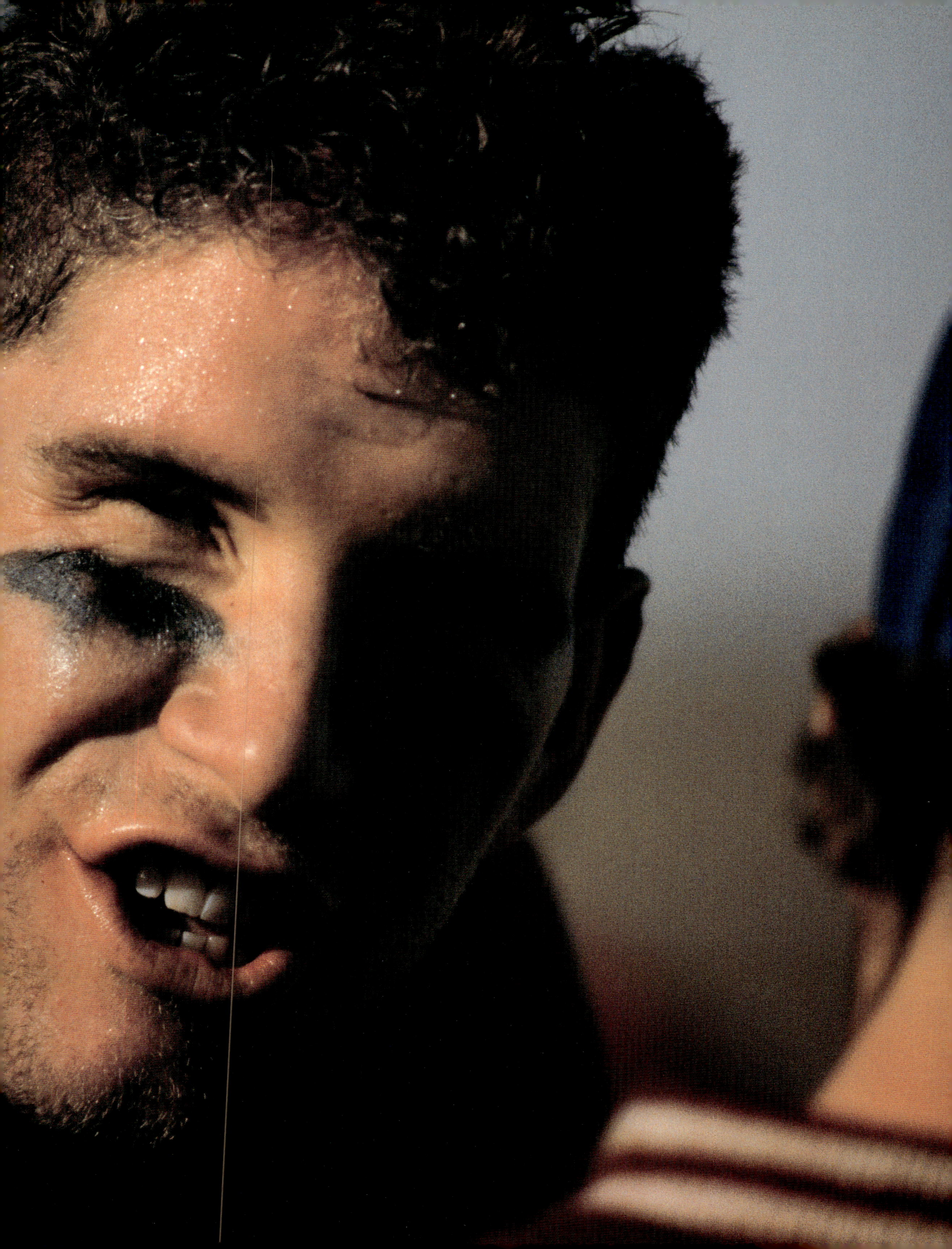

Pages 56-57. Cyclists whiz past golden-leafed trees that dot the campus in autumn.

Pages 58-59. Fighting Cardinal quarterback Drew Komlo of College Park, Md., readies for battle on the field at the Raymond A. DuFour Athletic Center. The 40-acre complex is named for a benefactor from the class of 1928, trustee emeritus and former football star.

Above. School of Nursing major Kellie Dunphy of Maple Glen, Pa., and University mascot, alias Joan Carlin, of Ardsley, N.Y., help rouse CUA football fans.

Right. President William J. Byron, S.J., joins Homecoming King Sean D. Mahaney of Akron, Ohio, and Queen Lourdes M. Casares of Coral Gables, Fla., psychology majors, on the sidelines to watch the Homecoming football game.

Say, this is some place.

President Theodore Roosevelt
during an impromptu campus visit in 1905

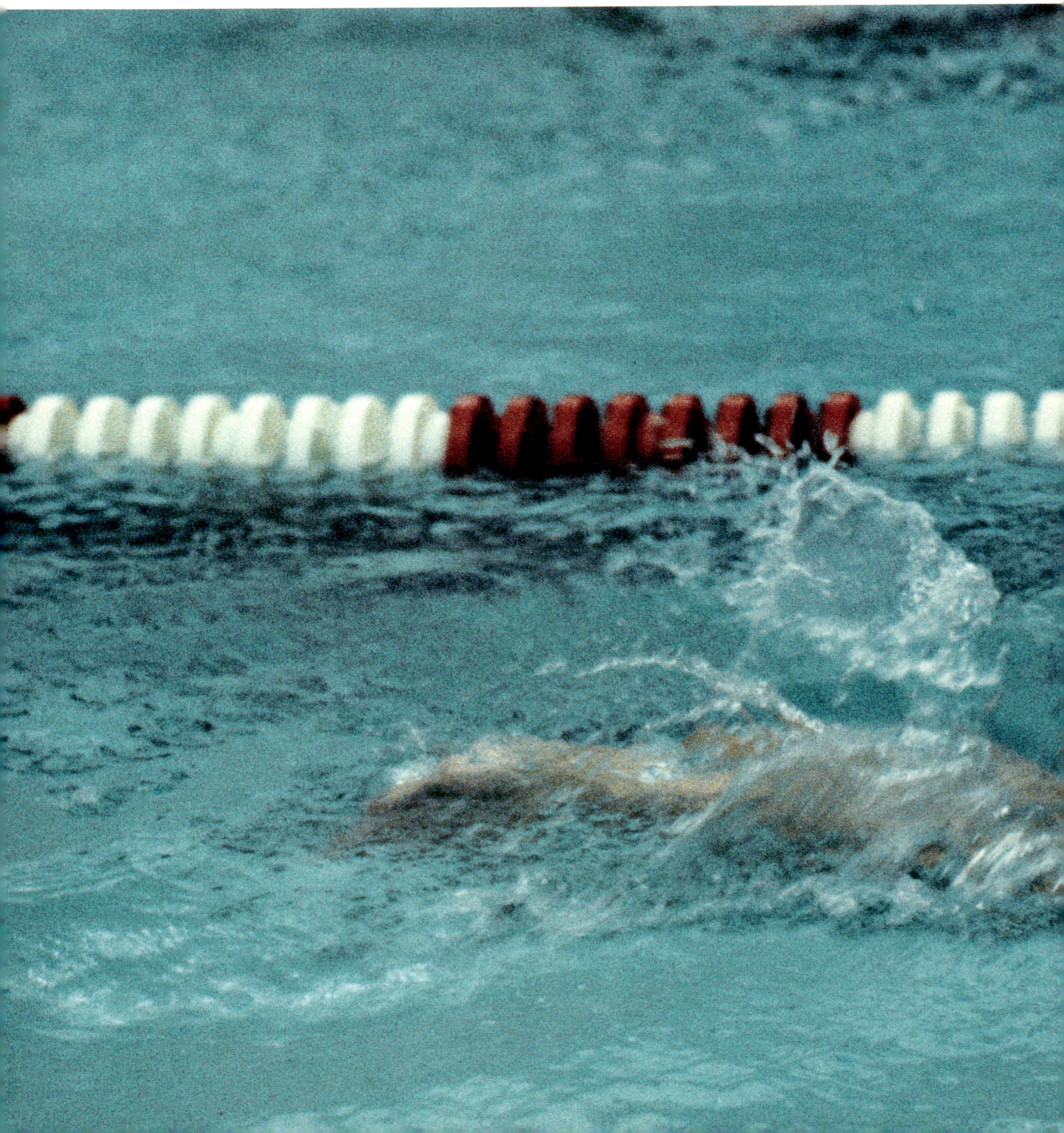

A member of the women's swim team competes at the athletic center's pool. CUA's women swimmers matched their male counterparts' success by winning nine meets without a loss during the 1989-90 season.

While studying literary theory, methodology and criticism at CUA, I began to realize the extent to which music encodes values, history and faith of my people.

Sister Thea Bowman, F.S.P.A.
M.A. '69, Ph.D. '72

Left. No matter what instrument a musician plays, talent, discipline, practice and proper techniques are essential. Distinguishing the music school is strong academic and professional training taught by a dedicated faculty in Washington, where opportunities abound.

Right. Music programs advance toward perfection in Ward Hall, built in 1934 and named after Justine Bayard Ward, whose estate endows liturgical music studies.

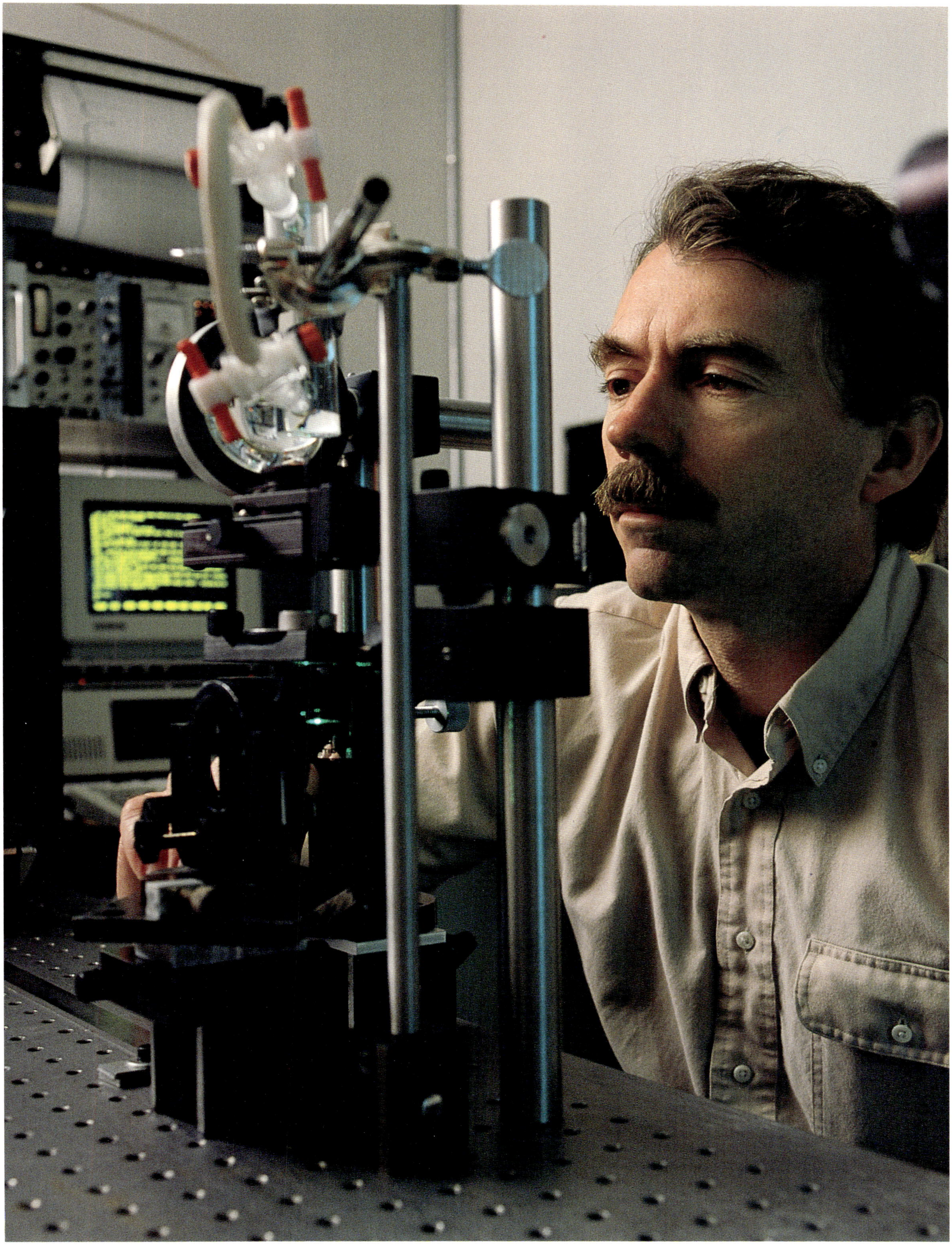

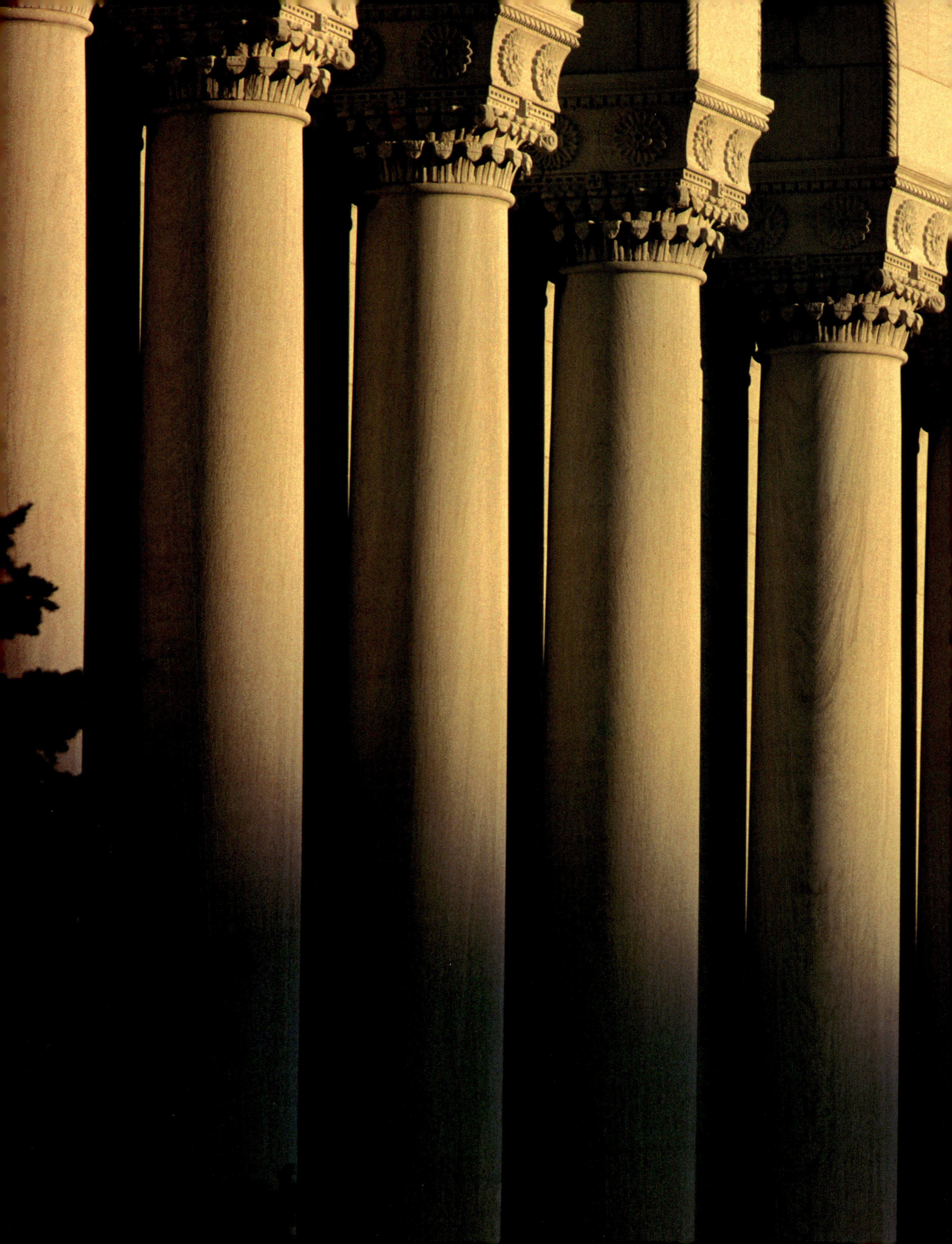

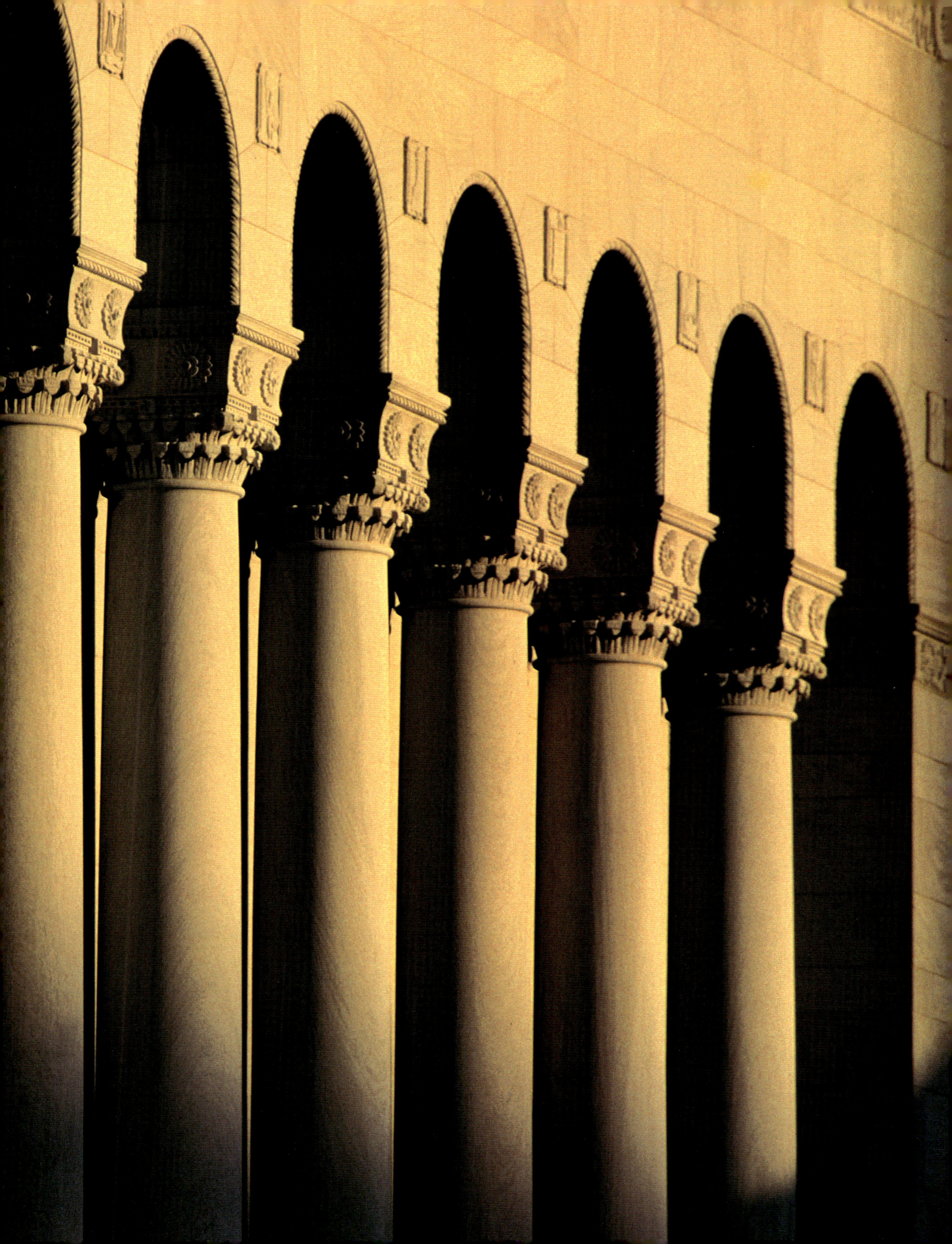

Pages 130-131. The stately Romanesque-style colonnade enhances the John K. Mullen of Denver Memorial Library, which houses more than a million volumes and outstanding collections in canon law, theology, philosophy and Semitic languages. The library has more than 200 manuscript collections focusing on the history of the U.S. Catholic Church, the American labor movement and American Catholic social history.

Mechanical engineering Professor Amr Baz, center, assists seniors Jorge Vazquez of Rio Piedras, Puerto Rico, left, and Mohd Z. Jasman of Kuala Lumpur, Malaysia, in a complex laboratory experiment.

To separate a protein into different components during a biochemistry experiment, Zaida Gomez of Ponce, Puerto Rico, injects the substance into a fast protein liquid chromatographer. She is a biology department research assistant and recipient of a Doctor of Arts degree in medical technology.

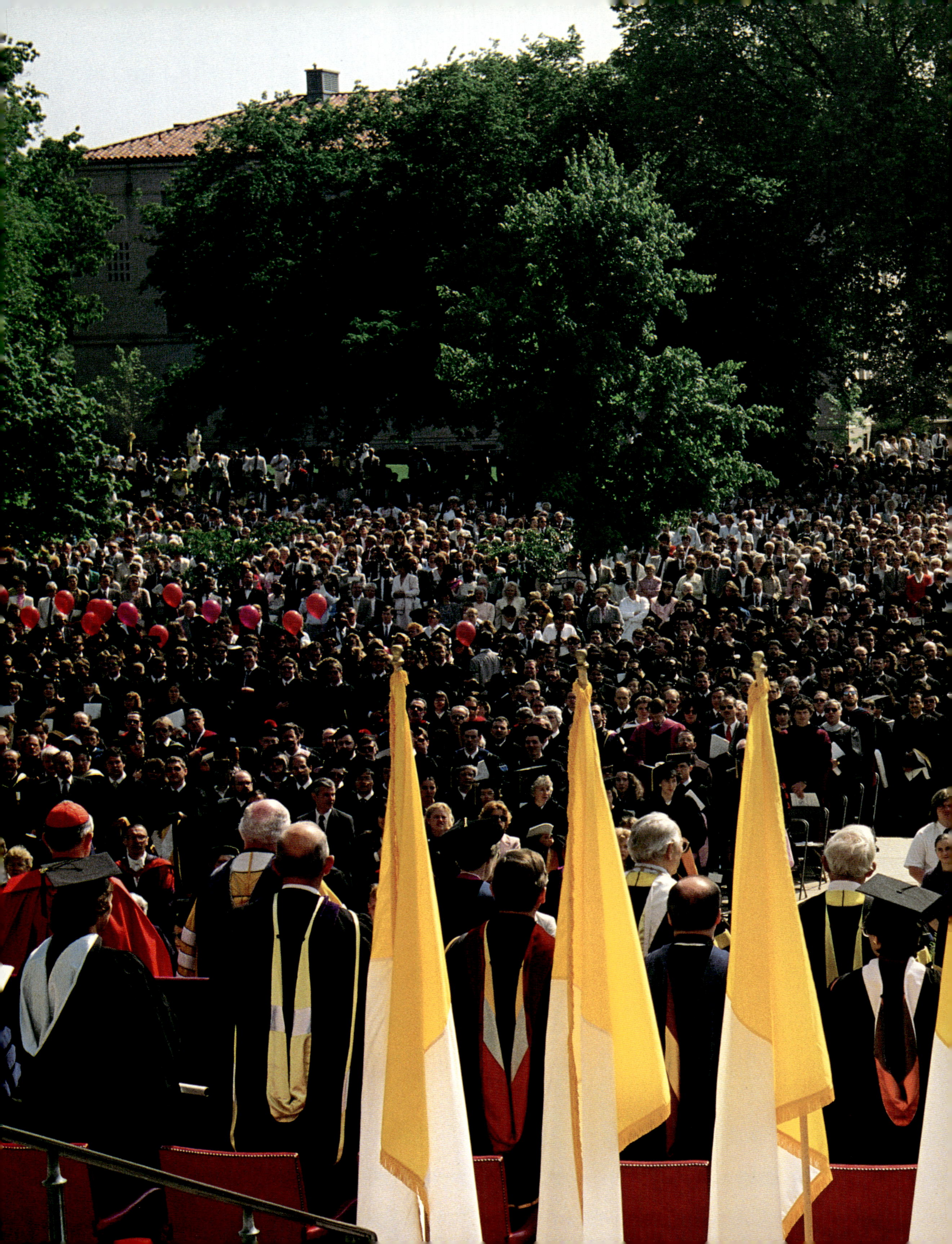

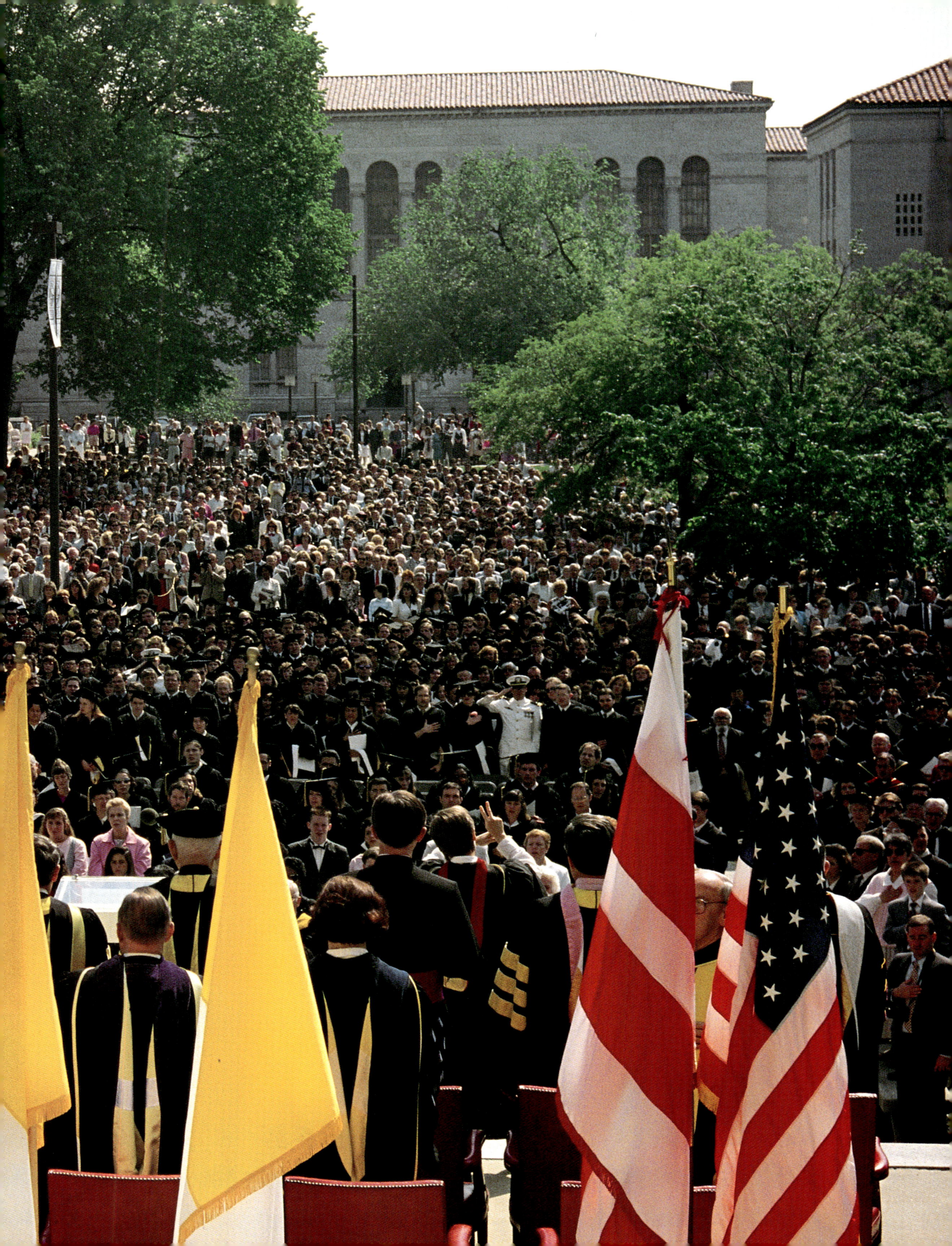

It gives me immense satisfaction to have the opportunity today—at this University which holds the unique position of uniting human and scientific teachings with those of theology—to share with you several thoughts on the extraordinary events we are witnessing in Europe, the repercussions of which will sweep across the whole system of international relations.

Prime Minister Giulio Andreotti of Italy
March 7, 1990
Campus Convocation

Pages 134-135. On a bright May morning, graduates, surrounded by families and friends, gather for the formal ceremony to signify a beginning on new paths. CUA confers about 1,600 undergraduate, graduate and law degrees annually.

Left. Associate Professor Sen Nieh, left, joins the graduation celebration of Seong Wong Lee of Korea, a 1989 mechanical engineering graduate, and his family.

Above. Commencement 1989 means sunshine and smiles to architecture graduates Mary Ellen Lynch of Chevy Chase, Md., and Denise Rothballer of Rye, N.Y.

I am so moved by this wonderful commencement that I have asked the chancellor of the University to let me express my deep thanks for the great honor which has been conferred upon me today. I am very happy to be on the platform with so many of my old friends.

President Franklin D. Roosevelt
Commencement 1933

Above. Graduation Day is a time for families and friends to celebrate with the graduates.

Right. With their brilliantly colored academic hoods exhibiting the diversity of educational backgrounds, faculty members share colloquial greetings as they gather for the joyous 1990 commencement procession.

138

Pages 140-141. New graduates adjust their hoods as soon as the University president announces the conferral of degrees.

Pages 142-143. "Broadway Night" features a boisterous performance of "Be a Clown." The highly praised event draws bigger crowds every year to see CUA students' professional achievements on the stage.

Page 144. Architectural features of McMahon Hall, a Richardson Romanesque-style building opened in 1895, include a curved-arch entry with granite columns. The building was designed by Baldwin and Pennington of Baltimore, known for B&O Railroad stations.

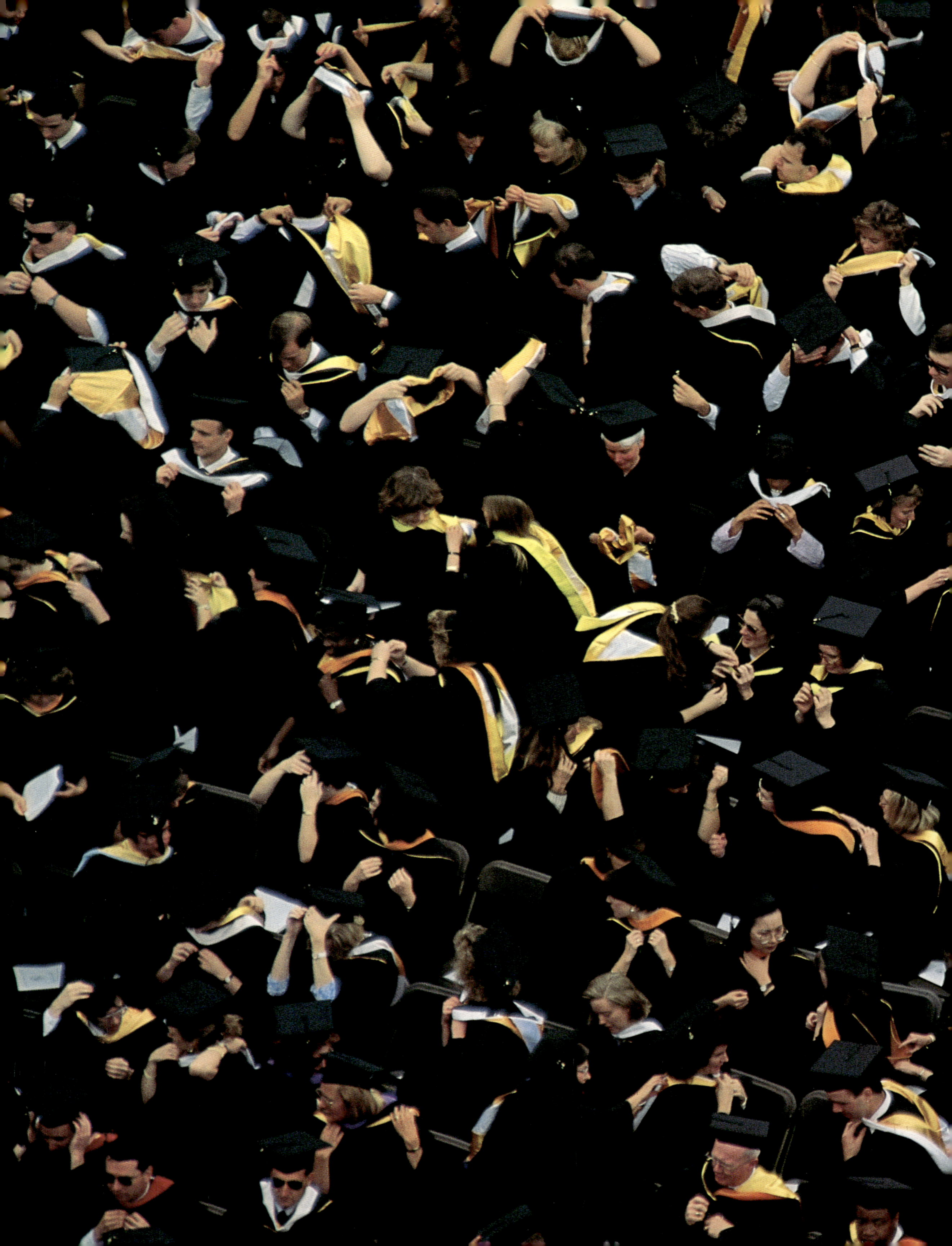

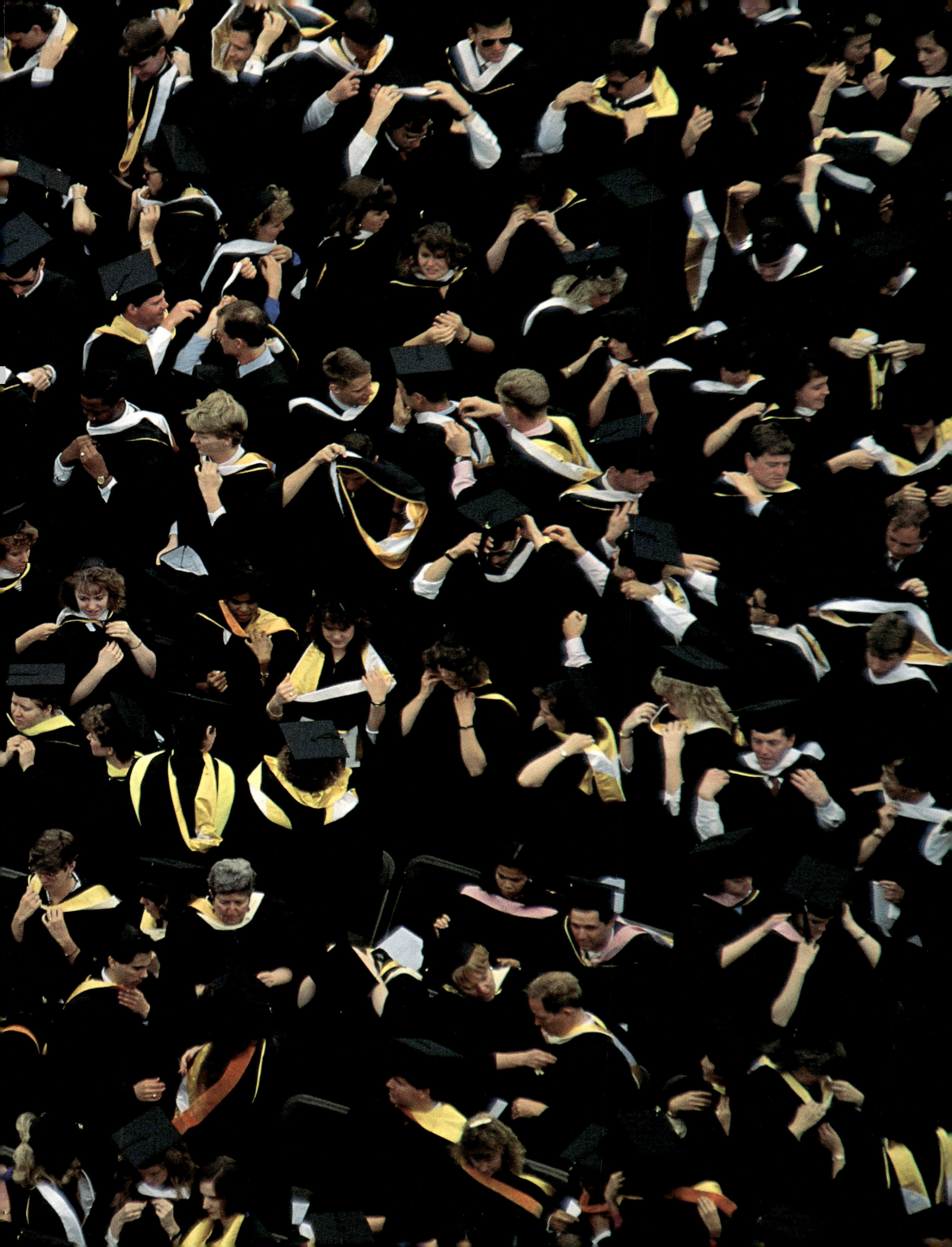

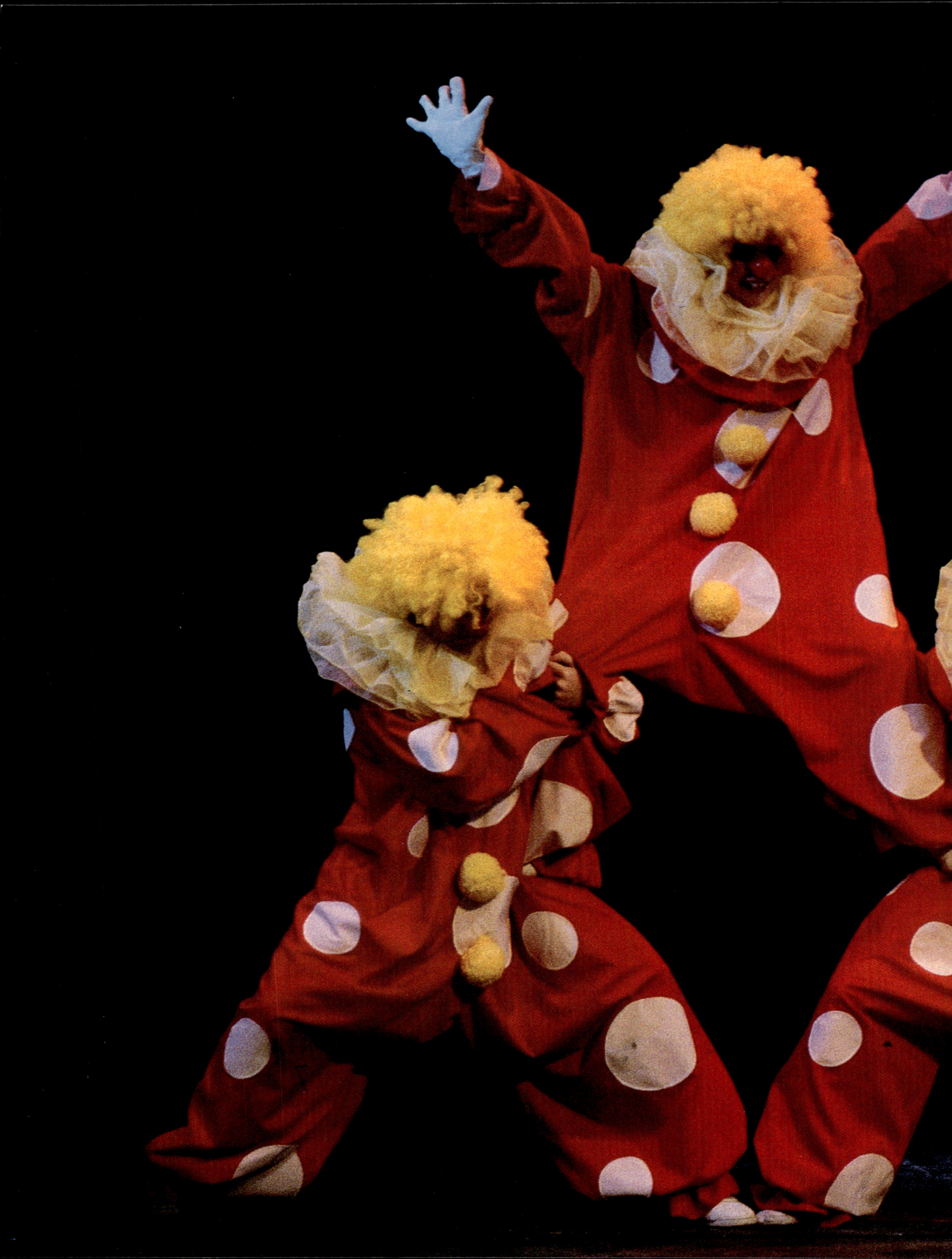

WITHDRAWN

MARIAN UNIVERSITY LIBRARY
INDIANAPOLIS, IN